A SHEWING OF GOD'S LOVE

The *Spiritual Masters* series:

St John of the Cross
The Mystical Doctrine of St John of the Cross
a selection introduced by R. H. J. Steuart, S.J.

Julian of Norwich
A Shewing of God's Love
the shorter version of *Sixteen Revelations of Divine Love*, edited by Anna Maria Reynolds

Bd Robert Southwell
Spiritual Exercises and Devotions
translated by P. E. Hallett

St Teresa of Avila
The Interior Castle
translated by E. Allison Peers

St Thomas Aquinas
Meditations and Readings for Lent
translated by Philip Hughes

A Shewing of God's Love

Julian of Norwich

Edited Anna Maria Reynolds

Sheed and Ward
London

 Nihil obstat J. M. T. Barton, Censor. *Imprimatur* E. Morrogh Bernard, Vicar General, Westminster 16 September 1957. Printed in Great Britain for Sheed and Ward Ltd, 6 Blenheim Street, London W1Y OSA, by Redwood Burn Ltd, Trowbridge and Esher.

TO OUR LORD GOD
WHO HAS IN US
HIS HOMELIEST HOME
AND
HIS ENDLESS DWELLING

CONTENTS

ACKNOWLEDGMENTS

We are indebted to Messrs. Burns Oates & Washbourne Ltd. for extracts from *The Ancrene Riwle* edited by M. B. Salu, and Messrs. Desclee & Cie, Tournai, for extracts from *A Treatise on Ascetical and Mystical Theology* by the Very Reverend A. Tanquerey, and translated by the Reverend H. Branderis. The frontispiece photograph is from a print kindly lent by Mrs. A. E. Kitchin. Copyright Hallam's Gallery, Norwich.

PREFACE

THIS edition of the Shorter Version of the *Revelations* of Julian of Norwich, intended primarily for devotional use, has been prepared from the unique fifteenth-century text as contained in British Museum Additional MS. 37790. Modern spelling, punctuation and paragraphing have been adopted, and chapter numbers and headings have been added.

While every effort has been made to preserve the idiom and vocabulary of the original, it has nevertheless been considered necessary in some instances, for the sake of clarity and ease in reading, to replace an obsolete word by a modern one, and to transpose or expand a phrase. Passages whose meaning is not clear have been interpreted in the light of the fuller exposition given in the Longer Version of Julian's book. Quotations from the Longer Version are modernized from the Paris manuscript.

The editor desires to acknowledge the help she has received from the Rev. D. Harford's edition of the Shorter Version, now for long out of print. She takes this opportunity of expressing her gratitude to all who have contributed in any way to her study of Julian. In particular she wishes to thank the authorities of the British Museum, Bibliothèque Nationale, and Westminster Cathedral Library for allowing her to examine their manuscripts of the *Revelations*. She wishes to convey her thanks to Professor R. M. Wilson of Sheffield University, Dr. A. C. Cawley of Leeds University, Dr. H. E. Allen, Miss Lillie Fenwick, and Miss C. Kilbride for their encouragement and help. She acknowledges her indebtedness to the Very Rev. Mgr. Canon J. Bradley for help with the philosophical background of the *Revelations*, to Father P. Molinari, S.J., for a greater understanding of Julian's spiritual doctrine, and to her Superiors and Sisters in religion for their constant inspiration, sympathy, and advice.

Finally she wishes to express her deep gratitude to Father J. Walsh, S.J., for his careful and enlightening revision of her translation of the text, and for all the practical help he has so kindly given.

Sister Anna Maria Reynolds, C.P.

INTRODUCTION

Manuscripts of The Revelations

Sixteen Revelations of Divine Love is an account of a series of visions shewn to its author, Julian, a recluse at St. Julian's Church, Norwich, in 1373, when she was thirty and a half years old.

Among the manuscripts of this remarkable work that have come down to us there is one, the oldest and shortest of them all, which stands apart from the others.[1] It is with this fifteenth-century manuscript that we are here chiefly concerned. It consists of two hundred and thirty-eight vellum folios, beautifully written in single columns of about thirty-two lines to a page, with initials in blue thickly laid on and flourished in red. On the first folio is a sixteenth-century owner's name. The manuscript bears also the bookplates of William Constable (d. 1791), member of an ancient Yorkshire Catholic family, and of Lord Amherst. It was bought by the British Museum from the latter's library in 1909. The *Revelations* takes up nineteen pages of the book, which contains twelve treatises altogether.

The complete later manuscripts contain about three times as much material as this oldest one. They begin with an account of the order in which the sixteen shewings were made and the subject-matter of each; and they end with a passage describing the meaning and purpose of the shewings. After the account of the Fourteenth Revelation there is included in the longer manuscripts (Chapters 44–63) additional material in the form of teaching on many points connected with the preceding fourteen revelations.

Julian herself informs us that she spent nearly twenty years pondering in prayer the meaning of the visions, during which time she received 'teaching inwardly' to help her to realize their full significance. But these lights in prayer were not extraordinary favours, they were not further 'revelations'; they were 'ordinary' actual graces granted by the Holy Spirit to help the recipient to grow in the knowledge and love of God.

The twenty-five rather brief chapters of the Shorter Version appear at first sight to be an abridged account of the Longer Version's eighty-six chapters. The more the two versions are studied and compared, however, the more one is inclined to believe that in the fifteenth-century manuscript is preserved a description of Julian's experiences as written soon after their occurrence in May 1373, while every detail was still fresh in Julian's mind, and before the fuller teaching referred to above had been received.

The version of the *Revelations* here presented in modernized form is, therefore, of the highest importance. It derives a peculiar interest and value from the fact that it presents us with an account of Julian's revelations written while her mind was still under the initial impact of the experience, an account which can be compared with the later, fuller, and (in some ways) more formal statement of the Longer Version. Moreover, as a spiritual document full of sound and consoling doctrine, it should be of value to all who desire to be 'Christ's Lovers'; as a concise account of Julian's teaching it will be welcomed by those who are already familiar with, and admirers of, the longer work; and as an introduction and companion to that longer book it is indispensable for serious students of unitive prayer in general, and of Julian's own experiences in particular. Finally it is hoped that the book may not be entirely without interest for the general student of medieval English literature.

The Author

Julian of Norwich lived through a stirring and creative, if critical, period in English history. Hers was the age of Crécy, Poitiers and Agincourt, of the Black Death, the Peasants' Revolt, and the rise of Lollardy. She saw four kings sit on the throne of England. She was a contemporary of Chaucer and Langland, of Walter Hilton and the author of *The Cloud of Unknowing*. The glories of the Decorated style as seen in Exeter Cathedral, parts of York Minster, Lincoln and Ely Cathedrals, must have been familiar to her; and echoes of the philosophical and theological arguments of the fourteenth-century Schoolmen may well have penetrated even to the seclusion of the anchorhold at St Julian's Church, Conisford, Norwich.

But Julian does not greatly concern herself with any of these things. Her book is a spiritual document intended for the help and consolation of all who desire to live in union with God. She is remarkably reticent even about herself; and in this respect both contemporary and later writers seem to have followed her lead, for few references to herself, and, apart from the extracts in the Westminster MS., none at all to her book, have come down to us.

From Chapter 2 of the longer text of her book

we learn that Julian was thirty and a half years old in May 1373, when the revelations occurred, so she must have been born towards the end of 1342. References to her in fifteenth-century wills tell us that she was a recluse at St Julian's and that she was still living in 1416. The prologue to the shorter text of the *Revelations* speaks of her as 'a devout woman', and Dame Margery Kempe of Lynn in her *Book* states that the anchoress was expert in spiritual matters and skilled in the art of giving 'counsel'.

This is the sum-total of our direct knowledge at present. We do not know if Julian was a nun before becoming an anchoress, or if she was already an anchoress when the shewings were granted to her. We do not even know if Julian was her own name: it could have been adopted from the church to which her anchorhold was attached.

Fortunately, however, these meagre details may be supplemented by information gleaned through a careful study of Julian's own writings and those of earlier and contemporary English literary figures. From these sources, indeed, it is possible to find out a good deal about the anchoress's character and personality, her manner of life as a recluse, and the quality of her spiritual experiences. It seems advisable to deal with each of these separately.

'*The First English Woman of Letters*'

'*Sixteen Revelations of Divine Love*, would be a remarkable book in any age; as a product of fourteenth-century England it is something of a miracle. To begin with, its author is a woman, a fact that at once challenged contemporary English convention, firmly set as that convention was against women's receiving mystical favours at all, and still more against their desiring to blaze them abroad, if such favours were actually experienced. Moreover, despite the profoundness and sublimity of its subject-matter, the *Revelations* is written in the most lucid and expressive of English prose, with just enough rhetorical device to place it unmistakably in the tradition of the *Ancren Riwle* and of Rolle. Most surprising of all, perhaps, the matter of this book, written in English by an anchoress of Norwich, has little in common with the works of these great spiritual writers to whose age and country she belonged: Rolle, Hilton, and the author of *The Cloud of Unknowing*; and no affinities whatever with the book of her famous contemporary and fellow-visionary, Margery Kempe of Lynn.'[2]

When describing the circumstances in which her visions were experienced, Julian alludes to herself as 'a simple creature, unlettered', and the precise significance to be attached to these plain words has exercised many scholarly brains. Mindful of the fact that St Catherine of Siena, renowned continental contemporary of Julian, never learnt to write, and that Blessed Dorothea of Prussia, also a contemporary of the Norwich recluse, is described in the *Acta Sanctorum* as 'almost illiterate'; and influenced too, no doubt, by Eileen Power's rather devastating summing up of the general standard of education among English religious women in the later Middle Ages,[3] some scholars strongly incline to a literal interpretation of Julian's words, and hold that the anchoress's educational attainments were just about the same as those of her illustrious sisters on the Continent.

Others, however, think it more likely that Julian is here speaking of herself with the humility characteristic of the saints, and that her words imply that she was no 'scholar'. This view is supported by the possibility of interpreting 'unlettered' as meaning 'ignorant of *Latin*', and by a remark made later in her book that she had teaching within her 'as it were the beginning of an A.B.C.', which does seem to suggest that the anchoress had at least mastered the art of reading.

Certain it is that her writings in no way suggest an untutored mind. Though it contains, apart from biblical sayings, but one direct quotation, the *Revelations* is nevertheless so full of scriptural allusion and imagery, so shot through with echoes of other spiritual writings, as to compel the belief that its author, through whatever medium, was familiar with the common stock of ideas in a vigorous mystical tradition, and with at least some of the classic expositions of those ideas.

By far the most important single literary influence discernible in the *Revelations* is the Bible, both Old and New Testaments. Whether her knowledge had come by reading or by hearing, Julian's familiarity with the language and thought of the Scriptures is truly remarkable. Occasionally it is revealed by a spontaneous use of direct quotation, usually short and sometimes inaccurate, as if she were relying on her memory; for example:

'And in the time of joy I might have said with Paul: "Nothing shall separate me from the charity of Christ." And in pain I might have said with St Peter: "Lord, save me, I perish!" ' (Ch. IX) More frequently it shows itself in her use of concepts adopted from the Scriptures and expanded by Julian. The Pauline writings, for example, provide two figures highly important for Julian's thought, especially in the Longer Version: the duality of man's nature (expressed in Rom. 7 : 15–25, 2 Cor. 4 : 16, etc.), and the image of the

Church as the Body of Christ (found in I Cor. 12 : 27; Rom. 12 : 5; Eph. 1 : 23; etc.); and it is claimed that in her *Revelations* one may see 'the continuity, and even the development', of the Johannine doctrine of Indwelling.[4]

But it is by her 'unconscious' use of Scripture, namely the clothing in biblical language of a theme not in itself biblical, and by her frequent use of scriptural phraseology, that Julian most clearly demonstrates her close familiarity with the text of the Bible, either in the Vulgate or in the vernacular. Almost every page of the *Revelations* is steeped in such biblical reminiscence. The following examples from the Shorter Version come at once to mind:

'So if any man or woman withdraw his love from any of his fellow-Christians, he loves right naught, for he loves not all . . .' (Ch. VI; cf. I John 4 : 8, 20)

'. . . I beheld continually a part of the Passion: contempt, spitting on, defiling of His body, buffeting His blessed Face . . .' (Ch. VIII; cf. Matt. 17 : 30; Luke 22 : 64)

'. . . see here how I allowed my side to be opened and my heart cloven in two, so that all the blood and water that was therein poured out.' (Ch. XIII; cf. John 19 : 34)

'I say not that I need no more teaching, for our Lord, with the shewing of this, has left me to Holy Church: I am hungry and thirsty and needy and sinful and frail . . .' (Ch. XIII; cf. Matt. 5 : 6; 25 : 42)

'. . . I am glad that thou art come to rest; for I have ever loved thee, and love thee and now thou lovest me.' (Ch. XIX; cf. Matt. 11 : 28–30)

Of non-biblical writings it is possible that Julian may have had access to passages from St Augustine, and Gregory's *Life of St Benedict.* There was an Augustinian friary in the very street where St Julian's church stood, and the writings of St Augustine may well have formed the subject of many a discourse with the friars, especially as his teaching on grace was one of the major controversial theological questions of Julian's day. The only direct non-biblical quotation in her book is from Gregory's *Life of St Benedict*, but there is no indication of how the anchoress came by it, though it may well have been through the Benedictines of the abbey at Carrow, in whose 'gift' the church of St Julian lay.

Of books in English current in the fourteenth century and likely to have been familiar to Julian, the works of Richard Rolle, the *Benjamin Minor* of Richard of St Victor, *The Cloud of Unknowing*, Hilton's *The Scale of Perfection*, and the *Mystical Theology* of Pseudo-Dionysius (whom she mentions by name in the

Longer Version), and, of course, the *Ancren Riwle*, are among the chief. Her *Revelations* contains some obvious, but probably unconscious borrowings from the latter book, which is not surprising, since the *Riwle* was such a popular 'text book' for intending anchoresses that it was still being copied as late as the fifteenth century, about two hundred years after its original compilation.

More surprising, at first sight, is the fact that parts of the Longer Version of Julian's book show some affinity with the writings of certain men on the Continent, notably the great Dominican, Eckhart. But when one recalls what an influence the Dominicans had in Norwich at this period, and the active trade relations that existed between Norwich and the Continent, one can understand how easily religious ideas current abroad might reach the ears even of a recluse.

The Bible; at least a nodding acquaintance with one or two of the Fathers; contemporary vernacular 'standard works of devotion'; some familiarity with the thoughts of continental theologians and mystics: not an unimposing achievement for an obscure 'devout woman' in the fourteenth century. Julian, moreover, made her own of what she heard or read, assimilated it and brought it forth again with humble assurance when the Holy Spirit stirred her thereto.

What of the form given by the anchoress to her account of her experiences? Is her prose worthy of the message it enshrines? Has she got 'style'?

Apart from two or three pages of graceful comment in Grace Warrack's edition of Julian's book, the prose of the *Revelations* has come in for very little notice even from those who have written enthusiastically about the subject-matter of her book. Evelyn Underhill in the *Cambridge Medieval History* refers to Julian as 'The first English Woman of Letters';[5] R. W. Chambers remarks, without illustration, that the prose of the *Revelations* is 'exceedingly beautiful';[6] Dom David Knowles writes of 'the simplicity and absence of all that is false or artificial' in the expression of her thoughts.[7] The rest is silence.

In view, therefore, of the 'excellent English prose which was being written in the first half of the fourteenth century, and the glorious English prose which we find in the second half',[8] it may be both useful and interesting to inquire how far the *Revelations*, also written in the fourteenth century, is worthy of the age which produced *The Form of Living*, *The Scale of Perfection*, and *The Cloud of Unknowing*.

Dr. Chambers has shown that the prose of these devotional works is in the direct line of a tradition deriving from the pre-Conquest homiletic prose of Ælfric and Wulfstan, through the *Ancren Riwle*, still being read and copied, as already mentioned, even in the fifteenth century. It is against this distinguished background of devotional writing that Julian's achievement must be considered. To appreciate the range, flexibility, and efficiency of Julian's prose, however, it must be remembered that the use of English for purposes other than devotional, for example in scientific documents, national chronicles or civic affairs, did not become general for more than half a century after the *Revelations* was finally composed, that is, until the middle of the fifteenth century.

A blending of traditional elements with personal characteristics gives to Julian's prose an indescribable vitality and charm. Alliterative phrases such as 'grace of God', 'worldly weal', 'truly taught', 'so gladsome and so ghostly', 'in weal and in woe', abound in her work. Their presence links the *Revelations* at once with earlier vernacular religious prose, while the ease and unobtrusiveness of their use make it clear that they have not been put in because of a prevailing fashion (even if one could imagine Julian being thus preoccupied with style).

An equally pervasive traditional element in her prose is the synonymous phrase, which in its simplest form consists of two synonyms or near synonyms joined by a conjunction. It is a very old device, much used in Anglo-Saxon prose. In the *Revelations* it is employed with remarkable success for emphasis and rhythmic effect, though again without the smallest trace of artificiality—indeed one scarcely notices the device until it is pointed out. Yet the number of such phrases, even in the Shorter Version, is large and their variety impressive: 'fleshly or earthly', 'wonder and marvel', 'feeble and frail', 'see and know', 'dimly and darkly', 'pain and travail', and so on.

Another characteristic of Julian's writings which once more reminds us that she is truly a child of her times, is the presence in it to a considerable degree of the figures and ornaments of rhetoric, so dear to the hearts of Englishmen in the latter half of the fourteenth century that Chaucer satirizes the fashion in his *Nun's Priest's Tale*. Julian is particularly partial to those figures based on repetition of word or clause and some of her most poignant and memorable sayings are couched in the language of the rhetoricians:

'We are His bliss. We are His meed. We are His worship. We are His crown.' (Ch. XII)

'No more than His love for us is broken because of our sins, no more will He that our love for ourselves or for our fellow-Christians be broken.' (Ch. XVIII)

'If I might suffer more, I would suffer more.' (Ch. XII)

'I will make all things well.
I shall make all things well.
I may make all things well,
and I can make all things well; and thou shalt see thyself that all things shall be well.' (Ch. XV)

Antithesis of words or of ideas gives point and vividness to Julian's teaching:

'For He who was highest and worthiest was most completely despoiled and most utterly humiliated.' (Ch. XI)

'For the passion was a deed done in time by the working of love; but the love was without beginning, and is, and ever shall be, without any end.' (ibid.)

'He said not: "Thou shalt not be tempested; thou shalt not be travailed; thou shalt not be distressed." But He said: "Thou shalt not be *overcome*."' (Ch. XXII)

'For many men and women believe that God is All-Mighty and *may* do all; and that He is All-Wisdom and *can* do all. But that He is All-Love and *will* do all—there they stop short.' (Ch. XXIV)

The immediate source of the rhetorical influence and the other traditional features discernible in the prose of the *Revelations* it is not possible to determine. The most likely explanation is that Julian became familiar with these devices indirectly, through the medium of sermons and the meditative reading of such vernacular prose works as the *Ancren Riwle*, so that when she set herself to write, their idiom and forms of expression came quite naturally to her mind.

To these inherited elements, however, the anchoress adds her personal contribution: a predilection for the concrete image, for convincing circumstantial detail, and for certain words; restraint in tone; and a delicate sense of rhythm and cadence which it is impossible to do full justice to in a modernized rendering of her book.

Julian's images are drawn from the homely happenings of everday life:

'His might [the fiend's] is all locked in God's hand.' (Ch. VIII)

'Sin is the sharpest scourge that any chosen soul may be beaten with.' (Ch. XVII)

'By this medicine [confession of sin] it behoves every sinful soul to be healed.' (ibid)

'Though he be healed, his wounds are still seen before God, though not as wounds but as tokens of worship.' (ibid)

Convincing circumstantial detail is Julian's speciality:

'I understood that she had received three wounds *with a sword in the neck* . . .' (Ch. I)

'I desired more bodily light *in order to have seen more clearly*.' (Ch. VIII)

'My mother who stood, *with others*, and beheld me, lifted up her hand to my face *to lock my eyes* . . .' (Ch. X)

'In my sleep, at the beginning, methought the fiend seized me by the throat and would have strangled me . . . Soon a little smoke came in at the door, with a great heat and a foul stench. I said: "*Benedicite! Dominus*—Is everything here on fire?" And I thought it was a bodily fire that would burn us to death; *I asked them that were with me if they noticed any stench*; they said no, they noticed nothing. I said: "Blessed be God!" for then knew I well it was the fiend . . .' (Ch. XXI)

Yet one remarks at the same time a restraint in tone and the omission of coarse realistic detail of the kind found not infrequently in earlier and contemporary vernacular devotional writing. Julian, like Jane Austen, possessed the rare gift of knowing what to leave out.

Again, her choice of words, though sometimes unexpected, is always expressive: 'a *soft* dread'; 'God shewed me what sin is, *nakedly* . . .'; 'the *drying* of Christ's flesh . . .' The anchoress is particularly attached to the words *homely*, *courteous*, and *courtesy*, the romance associations of the two latter words being sublimated to convey the exquisite delicacy, condescension, and attentiveness of God in His dealings with the soul.

It would be outside the scope of these introductory remarks to attempt the kind of detailed analysis of selected passages that is needed to bring out the variety, sensitiveness, and efficiency as a literary medium of Julian's prose. In the *Revelations* we see vernacular prose being used to narrate, to describe, to expound, to evoke emotion, and to convey philosophical truth—five important functions of prose in any age. The prose of Julian's book is not just barely adequate to its task, moreover; it is not merely competent, without ease or grace. 'Objectivity, concreteness and impersonality,' characteristic qualities of good narrative prose, according to Sir Herbert Read,[9] are found in every narrative passage of Julian's writings. Even when she is herself the central figure in what she narrates (as in the account of her illness, Ch. II) the tone is that of an impartial observer; there is a detachment in the manner of it that shows true artistic restraint.

As a descriptive writer, vividness and realism are Julian's most obvious characteristics. The opening paragraph of Ch. X is a good example, with its astonishingly accurate observation of the physical changes in the Face of the dying Christ, though much of the rhythmic beauty of the description has been unavoidably lost in the modernized version.

Ch. XIX, 'Concerning Prayer,' shows Julian's command of expository prose. The primary qualities of this chapter are clarity and forcefulness. The theme is stated in the opening sentence, elaborated in the following pages, and recapitulated by way of conclusion:

'And thus with prayers (as I have before said), and with other good works that are customary, according to the teaching of Holy Church, is the soul oned to God.'

The clarity is achieved partly by repetition, in slightly differing forms, of the theme of the chapter, and partly by simplicity of diction. Sentence structure, reinforced by alliterative phrases and balancing clauses, contributes to the point and precision of the explanation. Altogether it is a wonderfully lucid and accurate statement of the theology of prayer.

The Apostrophe to Sin (Ch. XXIII) furnishes an example of a very different kind of prose, one not common in the *Revelations*. Here the appeal is not to reason, but to the emotions. The passage, which is omitted in the Longer Version, may have been written at a time of intense sensible fervour. The denunciatory opening, reinforced by a rhetorical question, arrests the attention, which is held by the series of five parallel statements each ending with the refrain 'I saw thee not' or 'I saw not thee' (it is surely by a touch of genius rather than by accident that the form with the more lingering cadence comes at the beginning and end of the series). The climactic arrangement intensifies the cumulative effect of the repetition and generates the feeling of scorn for the 'naught' of sin that the apostrophe is intended to convey. After the slowing down of the rhythm at the final *I saw not thee*, it continues more gently, rises to a second, lesser, crescendo at *wilfully ends in thee* and stops short again, almost breathlessly, before concluding triumphantly on the well-placed *confounded*. After such an outburst the prayer *God shield us all from thee!* does not seem wholly unnecessary.

Finally, in her record of the content of the First Revelation (Ch. IV), we see Julian, with ease and in a conversational tone, give expression to profound philosophical truths about the goodness of God and the contingency of creatures:

'I saw that He is to us all-thing that is good and comfortable for our help. . . . And so in this sight I saw truly that He is everything that is good. . . .

'In this He shewed me a little thing, the quantity of a hazel nut. . . . I looked thereupon and thought: "What may this be?" And I was answered in a general way, thus: "It is all that is made." I marvelled how it could last, for methought it might suddenly fall to naught for littleness. And I was answered in my understanding: "It lasts and ever shall last because God loves it, and so hath all-thing its being through the love of God." '

The vocabulary of this chapter is rich and varied, including both simple and technical words; and the assured rhythm of *and so hath all-thing its being through the love of God* and *In sooth, the Maker, the Lover, the Keeper*, is maintained throughout, admirably suggesting that sense of security and steady serenity which is one of the chief charms of the writer.

It has been said of the subject-matter of Julian's book that its author is 'as original as a Christian writer can well be'. Yet it may be said with equal truth that she remains firmly entrenched in the religious traditions of her age. Julian, apparently without effort, preserves her own personality—even to the extent of an occasional humorous parenthesis such as the delightful aside in Ch. XXIII:

'After this the fiend came again, with his heat and with his stench. . . . Also I heard a bodily jangling and speaking as if it had been of two people (*and both, to my thinking, jangled at once, with great earnestness, as though they were holding a parliament*) . . .'

What an attractive, lovable personality is revealed to us in the pages of the *Revelations*! No dull, insensitive mind could have produced this book, with its eloquent presentation of God's love for man, and of His almost unbelievable 'homeliness' and 'courtesy' in dealing with the soul; with its clear teaching on prayer and spiritual living, and its profound thoughts on the problems of evil, suffering and predestination.

Of Rolle Dr. Allen writes: 'Rolle's English writings cannot be read without regret that he was cut off in his prime . . . the tantalizing promise of his English would suggest that he might have gone on to something which, as it is, our literature lacks: fine, truly medieval prose, in which by instinct the writer used both Anglo-Saxon stylistic ornaments and the modern idom of our language.'[10] The student of Julian's prose may be pardoned for suggesting that the Norwich recluse continued where the Hampole hermit left off. Not without reason has Julian been acclaimed as 'the First English Woman of Letters'.

The Recluse

'As in the early days of the Church it had been the custom for many to take the vow and receive the consecration of a virgin, while living at home or in retirement, so throughout the Middle Ages, besides the regular nuns . . . there existed a certain number of these recluses, living a strict and almost entirely immured life, dependent upon charity for support, and upon bishops or parish priest for spiritual direction.'[11]

Men as well as women embraced this solitary life, and many men and women proceeded to the stricter life of the recluse only after having first spent some years as priests, monks, or nuns.

It is surely paradoxical that Julian, most illustrious of the medieval recluses, has in the course of her writings but one possible reference to her vocation as a solitary: 'This place is prison; this life is a penance, and in the remedy He willeth that we rejoice. The remedy is that *our Lord is with us, keeping us.*' (Ch. 77) Not even the tiniest morsel of 'inside information' about her life in the anchorhold of St Julian's Church does she offer us. It is not from herself, but from contemporary documents, that we learn of her being a recluse, that she had at least one maidservant, and that she enjoyed a reputation for holiness.

For details as to what exactly becoming a recluse entailed, we must turn to works written long before Julian's day. There appears to have been no uniform, universal, authoritative 'Rule' for recluses, but aspirants to such a life, or their spiritual guides, could have recourse to one or all of the following documents:[12] *The Regula Solitariorum*, by a priest named Grimlaic, possibly to be identified with a ninth-century ecclesiastic of that name; the twelfth-century *De Vita Eremitica*, written by St Aelred, Abbot of Rievaulx, for his sister and circulated widely in Latin, and, later, in English; and the early thirteenth-century English *Ancren Riwle* or *Rule for Anchoresses*. The last-named work, of which the author is unknown, appears to have been compiled originally for the benefit of three sisters who, on the very threshold of life, had elected to follow the hard way of the recluse. From the number of copies of the *Riwle* made during the thirteenth century, and from the influence which it is known to have exercised on vernacular devotional prose and on other 'Rules' in the fourteenth and fifteenth centuries, it is evident that the popularity of the *Ancren Riwle* was immense and enduring.[13]

The way of life envisaged in this document, therefore, probably approximates quite closely to that lived by Julian in the seclusion of her Norwich anchorhold; almost certainly she was familiar with the text of the *Riwle*, as we have suggested above, while its moderation of tone and sound practicality would have commended themselves to her spirit.

In most cases the anchorholds of recluses were attached to churches, those occupied by women were necessarily so, to ensure that the anchoress could assist at Mass. As a rule one window of the anchorhold looked into the church, and the author of the *Ancren Riwle* reminds his readers of the respect due to the Blessed Sacrament: 'Do not hold a conversation with anyone through the church window, but reverence it because of the holy Sacrament which you can see through it' (p. 30).

The amount of space actually allotted to the occupant of an anchorhold appears to have varied considerably. It might consist simply of a single apartment, or have several rooms, like a modern flat. Sometimes, too, a piece of garden formed part of the enclosure, where the recluse could indulge in a little vegetable-raising, or simply enjoy the fresh air. Besides the window looking on to the Sanctuary, there was one communicating with the outside world, and a third to admit light. The *Ancren Riwle* warns anchoresses to be seldom seen at their windows: 'be as little fond of your windows as possible. Let them all be small, those of the parlour smallest and narrowest. Have curtains made of two kinds of cloth, a black ground with a white cross showing both inside and outside' (p. 21).

Though as a rule the inhabitant of the anchorhold was a solitary in the strict sense, occasionally, as with the little group for which the *Ancren Riwle* was written, several people might live as solitaries in the same building.

Even when the recluse occupied her cell alone, however, at least one extern had to be provided to look after her temporal welfare. Julian's maid, Sarah, and a former maid, Alice, are mentioned, with Julian herself, in contemporary wills. The *Ancren Riwle* recommends having two women, 'one always to stay at home, the other to go out when necessary' (p. 189), and it gives minute instructions on how they should be treated and how they should behave:

'As far as you are able,' the anchoress is told, 'be generous to them with food and clothes and other things which the needs of the body demand, even though you are strict and stern with yourselves' (p. 191). On the other hand, the maid is 'to do what she is told without grumbling, and let her ears always be alert to hear her mistress. Let neither of the women', adds the *Riwle*, 'bring to or carry from her mistress any idle tales or news, nor exchange them with each other. . .' (p. 189).

For the provision of food and clothing for herself and her maids the recluse might rely on alms, endowments, or on private means. The practice of the spirit of poverty is urged by the author of the *Ancren Riwle*: 'no anchoress should take from others more than she reasonably needs. With what, then, can she be openhanded? She must live on alms as frugally as she possibly can, and not acquire things in order to give them away' (p. 184).

The vow of poverty is not mentioned, however: 'I advise that anchoresses should only make profession, that is, make solemn promises, in three matters,' says the *Riwle*: 'obedience, chastity, and stability of abode' (p. 3). This last is considered of very great importance: 'for whoever undertakes a thing, promising God that she will carry it out as if it had been commanded, binds herself by that promise, and sins mortally if she breaks it of her own free will' (ibid.).

The official ceremony of enclosure was sufficiently symbolic and impressive to bring out the significance of the step about to be taken by the intending recluse. A preliminary examination of the candidate's fitness was made, usually by an ecclesiastical superior appointed for the purpose by the bishop. If he was satisfied that the postulant possessed the necessary qualities of soul, mind, and body, a date was appointed for her solemn enclosure. Details of the ceremony differed in different parts of the country, but its essence remained the same, as with the profession ceremonial of religious orders and congregations in modern times.[14]

In all versions of the rite the postulant attended Mass on the day of her enclosure;

sometimes a Requiem Mass was stipulated, sometimes this was left to the choice of the officiating ecclesiastic. The garb of a recluse which was about to be assumed was blessed, and at some point in the ceremony, either during the Mass or immediately afterwards, the candidate read a formula of profession as a recluse. There followed the second half of the rite of enclosure. The intending recluse was led in procession to the anchorhold awaiting her, at the entrance to which she was left standing while the officiating cleric entered and blessed it. The postulant was then bidden to enter, the door was made fast, and the procession repaired once more to the church where prayers were asked for the newly interred recluse. In the Exeter rite the whole service strongly resembled an actual burial service: the In Paradisum was chanted as the postulant walked into the anchorhold, and the prayers for the commendation of a departed soul were said over the prostrate body of the newly-enclosed; finally the bishop, after everybody else had left the enclosure, bade the recluse in holy obedience to rise up and to spend in obedience what remained to her of life.

The occupant of the anchorhold was now officially 'dead to the world'. How did she set about living, ever more intensely, to Christ? For that, it must never be forgotten, was the primary reason why the medieval man or woman entered upon the hard and, humanly speaking, forbidding life of a recluse. Even Julian could write 'This place is *prison*. This life is a *penance*.' But she could add, with a conviction born of personal experience: 'in the remedy He willeth that we rejoice. The remedy is *that our Lord is with us, keeping us*.' When she wrote these words Julian had reached an advanced stage of union with God; we may well wonder if her fellow-recluses made an equally rapid ascent, and what spiritual weapons they employed in order to remove the obstacles to divine union.

To the latter question the *Ancren Riwle* provides a very full answer. The first of its eight parts or 'books' is taken up with minute directions about the prayers, liturgical and private, to the saying of which the recluse was chiefly to devote herself. The second part deals with the keeping of the heart; it is divided into five chapters, corresponding to the five senses which 'guard the heart like watchmen'. In the third part an exposition is given of the verse 'I am become like a pelican in the wilderness'. Fleshly and spiritual temptations, with the remedies against them, form the subject of the fourth part. The fifth part deals with Confession; the sixth, with penance. The seventh is concerned with purity of heart: why one ought and should love Jesus Christ, and the hindrances to this love. The eighth part is devoted entirely to the regulating of external matters: food, clothing, relations with the outside world, etc.

The author of the *Riwle* strongly enjoins the observance of silence. Silence was to be kept by the anchoress during the greater part of the day; on Fridays and for several days of the week in the penitential seasons this silence should be complete and unbroken. Strict silence was likwise enjoined for each day of Holy Week. But this did not mean, of course, that necessary instructions could not be given to the waiting-maid, still less that a stranger in search of 'ghostly counsel' should be sent away unconsoled; for the giving of such spiritual comfort was a most important duty of the medieval recluse.

The anchoress was not expected to eat her bread in idleness and silence, however:

'In the solitary life, with its strenuous religious exercises,' writes Miss R. M. Clay, 'it was at once a duty and a recreation to read much, to write, and (when gifted) to practise some handicraft.'[15] Manual work was advocated even when it was not necessary as a means of earning a living. Needlework was, of course, a craft much practised by the anchoress.

'I would rather have you do the plainer kinds

of needlework,' declares the author of the *Ancren Riwle*, '. . . cut out and sew and mend church vestments and garments for the poor. . . . None of you must make lace with a frame, either out of generosity or as paid work. I do not forbid you to make a narrow lace with which to edge surplices or albs; but let no one make other edgings, especially not elaborate ones, unless there is some great need' (p. 187). A little later, he warns his anchoresses that they must not let themselves drift into being schoolmistresses, turning the anchorhold into a schoolhouse. An anchoress, the writer of the *Riwle* thinks, 'ought to give her attention to no one but God, though she may on her director's advice, give help and guidance in learning' (p. 188). Miss Clay remarks that 'Recluses were eager for instruction', and notes a number of 'literary recluses' from the twelfth to the sixteenth centuries.[16] Roughly contemporary with Julian there was the Monk Solitary of Farne, who has left some Latin writings which may prove of considerable interest for the student of fourteenth-century mysticism.

Among other writers or 'book-lovers' who were also recluses, may be noted Brother John Lacy, 'the scribe illuminator of the Blackfriars, Newcastle-upon-Tyne', who produced a series of devotions as well as extracts from other spiritual books. Miss Clay describes Lacy as 'an indefatigable scribe' the one hundred and fifty-one folios of whose codex are wrought on both sides of the vellum, their borders decorated with floral designs. A little later than this northern Dominican (he finished writing in 1434), we find a southern Carthusian, John Dygoun, Master of Arts and Bachelor of Civil and Common Law, who was enclosed in 1435 beside the House of Bethlehem at Sheen. He is the first known English scribe of the spiritual classic familiar to every devout Christian as the *De Imitatio Christi*. Then there is, almost a century later, the celebrated Simon Appulby of London Wall, who produced a volume of prayers and meditations which was printed by Wynkyn de Worde; and finally 'the scholarly Benedicta Burton', the last anchoress of Polesworth, Warickshire, whose autograph has been found in a Latin textbook on education now known to have been printed at Basle in 1541.

Very important, too, are the books which, like the *Ancren Riwle*, were written not by recluses but for them. Richard Rolle's *The Form of Living*, for instance, among other English works, was written expressly for Dame Margaret Kirkby, a nun of Hampole, on the occasion of her enclosure as a recluse;[17] Rolle gives a characteristic and comprehensive account of his spiritual experiences. Hilton's *The Scale of Perfection* appears likewise to have been composed for an anchoress (a 'Ghostly sister in Jesus Christ') as we see from the opening chapter with its reference to 'a bodily enclosing' being a means the better to come to a 'ghostly enclosing'.

∽

'The Golden Age of the English Recluse' is said to have coincided roughly with the period 1225–1400.[18] Decay appears to have begun with the second quarter of the fifteenth century, though many anchorholds, including that at St Julian's, retained a succession of recluses well into the sixteenth century. With the change of religion and the dissolution of the monasteries the anchorhold as an institution inevitably declined, but 'Only with the Council of Trent and its legislation regarding the enclosure of convents did the type disappear from Europe'.[19]

Some hard things have been said and written about the life of the medieval recluse and those who embraced it; to the material-minded and the self-centred such an undertaking must always remain not only a mystery, but a scandal. It may be true that some recluses, like Judas, used their privileged position to betray their Master. Yet a way of life which in its beginning inspired the burning sincerity of the *Ancren Riwle*, and which in its maturity moulded the woman who left to posterity *Sixteen Revelations of Divine Love*, cannot but inspire admiration and respect.

The Mystic

As a personal record of alleged mystical experiences the *Revelations* calls for explanation and comment, since any claim to greatness made for its author must rest chiefly on two assumptions, the soundness of its mystical doctrine and the excellence of the prose in which that doctrine is expressed.

Was Julian a genuine mystic?[20] Before trying to answer this vital question some brief clarification of terms is necessary.

'Mysticism' is a word of many meanings nowadays. Here, however, by 'mysticism' is to be understood orthodox Christian mysticism, that is to say, 'the way of approach to God consequent upon a conviction that an immediate union between God and the soul is possible in this life'. This way of approach to God is by means of 'extraordinary states of prayer, and divine, often quasi-miraculous, operations upon the soul'.[21]

∽

Prayer may be either vocal or mental. Vocal prayer is that which is made by using some approved form of words which is read or recited; mental prayer is that which is made without employing a set form of words. The substance of 'ordinary' mental prayer lies in the activity of the soul itself: its acts of memory, understanding and will, while the operation of the Holy Spirit (without which all prayer is impossible)[22] is not perceived or 'felt' by the soul. In the advanced stages of this kind of prayer the activity of the soul is simplified and is reduced, more or less, to acts of love ('affective prayer'); the operation of the Holy Ghost is correspondingly intensified.

In 'extraordinary' or mystical prayer the Holy Spirit 'becomes the dominant partner'. His presence in the soul is 'felt' (experienced), while the soul itself is reduced under this action to a certain passive state. The peak of this kind of prayer is transforming union, when, in the words of St John of the Cross: 'on either side there is made surrender by total possession, of the one to the other with a certain consummation of union of love, wherein the soul is made Divine and becomes God by participation, in so far as may be in this life'. (*Spiritual Canticle*, Stanza XXII)[23]

Mystical prayer or infused contemplation has been described as a 'progressive taking hold of the soul by God, freely permitted by the soul itself'.[24] Although, because of differences in temperament and character, it is not the same in all persons who experience it, yet there seems to be a certain unity of pattern discernible which has enabled spiritual writers to classify the principal stages traversed by the mystics. The following division of infused contemplation into four degrees is based on the combined teaching of St Teresa and St John of the Cross.

'The various degrees are marked by a greater and greater hold of God on the soul. 1. When He takes possession of the subtile *point of the soul*, letting the lower faculties and the senses free to exercise their natural activity, we have the *prayer of quiet*. 2. When He seizes all the interior faculties, leaving merely the exterior senses to their own activity, we have the *full union*. 3. If He takes possession at the same time of the interior faculties and of the exterior senses we have *ecstatic union* (spiritual espousals). 4. Lastly, once He extends His hold over all the internal faculties and this, no longer in a transitory manner but in a *stable* and *permanent* fashion, we have the *spiritual marriage*.

'Such are the four degrees of contemplation according to St Teresa. St John of the Cross adds to these the *nights*, or *passive* trials; but the first night is but a species of quietude, *arid* and *crucifying*; the second night comprises the *sum-total* of trials, which precede the spiritual marriage and which are found in the full union and in the ecstatic union.'[25]

Extraordinary mystical phenomena such as visions and revelations frequently accompany infused contemplation, especially after the soul has reached the stage of ecstatic union. In orthodox Catholic mysticism, however, the importance attached to such phenomena is very limited indeed, the essence of mysticism being the union of the soul with God, not visions and revelations. Visions are supernatural perceptions of some object naturally invisible to man. They are revelations only when they disclose hidden truths. Such experiences are not necessarily of divine origin; they can be the result of diabolical agency or the fruits of neurosis and hysteria. However, it is possible to ascertain the cause of such phenomena by examining their effects. Hysterical neurosis can usually be detected by the content of the communications and their effect on the recipient and on those to whom they are made known.

Since the time of St Augustine theologians and spiritual writers have agreed in classifying visions as corporeal, imaginative, and intellectual.[26] Corporeal visions are those in which the senses perceive some real object that is naturally invisible to man. Imaginative visions are those produced in the imagination by God or by the Angels, either during sleep or while one is awake. Intellectual visions are those in which the mind perceives a spiritual truth without the aid of sensible impressions.

The great mystics are unanimous in teaching that one should neither desire nor ask in prayer for these extraordinary favours since they are not necessary means to divine union and are not, in themselves, any guarantee of personal holiness.

Such, in briefest outline, is the nature of the mystical experience. Throughout the history of the Church many of her members, men and women, have been called to serve God in this way, and not a few of them have, like Julian, left written accounts of their spiritual ascent.

∽

Our only source of information about Julian's revelations is the anchoress's own accounts of her experiences in the two versions of her book. From these we learn that the shewings were made on May 8th (or May 13th, according to the Paris manuscript) in the year 1373, when Julian was in her thirty-first year. She had been grievously ill and had received the last rites of the Church when she was suddenly and completely cured. At this point the series of revelations began, with the visions of the Crowning of our Lord with Thorns. It was about four o'clock in the morning.

Fifteen shewings followed in succession, lasting 'until it was noon of the day or later'. The sixteenth shewing was made on the following night, 'which sixteenth was conclusion and confirmation to all the fifteen,' says Julian in the Longer Version. (Ch. 66)

The opening chapter of the Longer Version gives a brief survey of the content of these revelations:

ꟹ

The *First* is of His precious crowning with thorns.
The *Second* is of the discolouring of His fair Face, in Tokening of His dearworthy Passion.
The *Third* is that our Lord God All-Mighty, All-Wisdom and All-Love . . . doeth and worketh all things that are done.
The *Fourth* is the scourging of His tender body, with plenteous shedding of His precious blood.
The *Fifth* is that the fiend is overcome by the precious Passion of Christ.
The *Sixth* is the worshipful thanking of our Lord God in which He rewardeth all His blessed servants in heaven.
The *Seventh* is often-times feeling of weal and of woe.
The *Eighth* is the last pains of Christ and His cruel dying.

The *Ninth* is of the liking which is in the Blessed Trinity of the hard Passion of Christ.
The *Tenth* is that our Lord Jesus sheweth by love His blessed Heart even cloven in two.
The *Eleventh* is an high ghostly shewing of His dearworthy Mother.
The *Twelfth* is that our Lord is all-sovereign Being.
The *Thirteenth* is that our Lord God wills that we have a great regard for all the deeds which He hath done . . .
The *Fourteenth* is that our Lord God is ground of our beseeching . . .
The *Fifteenth* is that we shall suddenly be taken from all our pain and from all our woe, and of His goodness we shall come up above where we shall have our Lord Jesus to our meed . . .
The *Sixteenth* is that the Blessed Trinity, our Maker in Christ Jesus our Saviour, endlessly dwelleth in our soul . . . and we shall not be overcome by our Enemy.

∽

All the teaching contained in the revelations was conveyed to her, declares Julian, in 'three parts. That is to say: by the bodily sight, and by words formed in my understanding, and by ghostly sight.' (Ch. XXIII) These 'three parts' correspond to the classification of visions as corporeal, imaginative, and intellectual, mentioned above.

A study of the *Revelations* leaves one convinced that the anchoress of Norwich was a true mystic. She certainly was no neurotic; the healthy commonsense and sturdy optimism of her book show that. Neither was she a 'devil's disciple'; this the sublime holiness of her doctrine amply proves. Although her book is not a formal treatise on prayer but a personal narrative set down for the benefit of her fellow-Christians, it contains, scattered here and there throughout its pages, a body of teaching on prayer and contemplation which corresponds to that of the classic spiritual writers of the West: Cassian, Gregory, Bernard, Anselm, and the Victorines. In fact the main lines of the development of contemplative prayer as worked out in the authoritative expositions of St Teresa (1515–1582) and St John of the Cross (1543–1591), themselves heirs to the accumulated mystical wisdom of the Middle Ages, are plainly discernible in Julian's book.

∽

Julian, for instance, distinguishes explicitly between 'ordinary' prayer ('seeking') and infused or mystic contemplation ('beholding'). She insists, but with gentleness and with the emphasis on positive measures, on the need for absolute self-renunciation on the part of those who desire to live contemplatively:

'. . . of this needs every man and woman who desires to live contemplatively to have knowing, that they should like to naught all things that are made for to have the love of God who is unmade. For this is the cause why they that are preoccupied wilfully with earthly business and ever more seek after worldly weal are not His in heart and in soul here: *they love and seek their rest in this thing that is so little, wherein is no rest*, and know not God who is All-Mighty, All-Wise and All-Good. For He is very rest.' (Ch. IV) Her prayer progresses from the prayer of quiet to the prayer of full union. Although Julian makes no reference to the spiritual marriage, she speaks at some length of the felt presence of the Blessed Trinity in her soul which presupposes this supreme degree of union. This is the prayer described in St Teresa's *Seventh Mansion*. 'Once the soul has been introduced into this mansion,' says Tanquerey, 'the Three Persons of the Most Blessed Trinity manifest themselves to it in an intellectual vision, and they come directly upon it as in a cloud of extraordinary brightness. The Three Divine Persons manifest themselves as distinct, and by a wonderful communication of knowledge, the soul sees with absolute certitude that all Three Persons are but one substance, one power, one knowledge, one God.'[27] And St Teresa herself writes: 'so that what we hold by faith the soul may be said here to grasp by sight, although nothing is seen by the eyes, either of the body or of the soul, for it is no imaginary vision. Here all three Persons communicate Themselves to the soul and speak to the soul and explain to it those words which the Gospel attributes to the Lord—namely, that He and the Father and the Holy Spirit will come to dwell with the soul which loves Him and keeps His commandments.' (*Castle*, VII, i)[28]

Julian's account of her own experience of this high favour is given in the Shorter Version as well as in the Longer Version of her *Revelations*, so she must have reached the supreme degree of Transforming Union while still a comparatively young woman:

'. . . our Lord opened my ghostly eyes and shewed me my soul in the midst of my heart, I saw my soul as large as if it were a kingdom, and from what I saw therein, methought it was a worshipful City.

'In the midst of this City is seated our Lord, true God and true man: beautiful in person and tall of stature—the worshipful, highest Lord; and I saw Him in majesty covered with glory. He sits in the very centre of the soul, in peace and rest, and rules and cares for heaven and earth and all that is. The Manhood, with the Godhead, sits in rest, and the Godhead rules and directs without any instrument or busy-ness; and my soul is blessedfully possessed by the Godhead that is Sovereign Might, Sovereign Wisdom, Sovereign Goodness.'

She also refers, but with characteristic cheerfulness, to the Nights of the Senses and of the Spirit, through which souls called to the spiritual nuptials usually pass.

The anchoress's attitude to visions is equally sound. She does not pray for these extraordinary graces and is not puffed up with pride when they come to her unsolicited. She is at first sceptical rather than credulous of their genuineness and repeatedly expresses her entire submission to the Church on all matters connected with the content of her revelations:

'*Because of the shewing I am not good, but only if I love God the better*, and so may, and so should, each one do who sees it and hears it with good will and true intent. . . . I am certain I saw it for the profit of many another, for in truth it was not shewed me that God loves me better than the least soul that is in grace; I am certain *there are full many who never had shewing nor sight but of the common teaching of Holy Church and who love God better than I. . . .*' (Ch. VI)

She returns again and again, even in the Shorter Version, to this matter of the all-importance of the 'common teaching of Holy Church'.

'I say not that I need no more teaching,' she says in Ch. XIII, 'for our Lord, with the shewing of this, *has left me to Holy Church*: I am hungry and thirsty, and needy and sinful and frail, and wilfully submit myself to the teaching of Holy Church, with all my fellow-Christians, unto the end of my life.'

Julian, clearly, does not belong to the type of soul of whom St John of the Cross writes:

'. . . the soul is so occupied with these things of sense that, as it is inclined to them by nature . . . it has only to observe in its confessor, or in some other person, a certain esteem and appreciation for them, and not merely will it at once conceive the same itself, but also, without its realizing the fact, its desire will become lured away by them. . . . And hence arise many imperfections, at the very least; for the soul is no longer as humble as before. . . .' (*Ascent II*. xiii)

Later, speaking of all who 'mightily and meekly and worshipfully receive the preaching and teaching of Holy Church', she concludes, 'all those who seek in this way shall succeed, for they seek God'. (Ch. XVI)

Has Julian's spiritual teaching any relevance for twentieth-century seekers after union with God? What are its characteristic notes? In the last chapter of the longer version of her book Julian herself tells us the meaning and purpose of the shewings, as taught her by Christ in response to her frequently expressed desire to know their significance.

'And XV years afterwards, and more, I was answered in ghostly understanding, saying thus: What! Wouldst thou know thy Lord's meaning in this thing? Know it well. Love was His meaning. Who shewed it thee? Love. [What shewed He thee? Love.][29] Wherefore shewed He it to thee? For Love. Hold thee therein. Thou shalt know more in the same, but thou shalt never know therein other thing without end.

'Thus was I learned that Love is our Lord's meaning. And I saw full surely in this, and in all, that ere God made us He loved us; which Love was never slaked, nor ever shall be. And in this Love He hath done all His works. And in this Love He hath made all things profitable to us. And in this Love our life is everlasting. In our making we had beginning; but the Love wherein He made us was in Him from without beginning: in which Love we have our beginning. And all this shall we see in God without end.'

Her spiritual message, with its insistence on God's inexpressibly tender love for His creatures in whom He condescends to have 'His homeliest home and His endless dwelling' generates a joyous, childlike, trustful love that is sorely needed by souls today. Julian's optimism is infectious:

'See! I am God,' says Christ in the Third Revelation, 'See! I am in all thing. See! I do all things. See! I never lift my hands off my works, and never shall, without end: See! I lead all thing to the end I ordain it to from without beginning, by the same Might, Wisdom and Love that I made it with: *How should anything be amiss*?' (Longer Version, Ch. 8)[30]

Prologue by the Scribe

Here is a vision shewn by the goodness of God to a devout woman whose name is Julian. She is a recluse at Norwich and is living yet in this year of our Lord 1413. In this vision are full many comfortable and most moving words unto all those who desire to be Christ's lovers.

I

JULIAN'S THREE DESIRES

I DESIRED three graces by the gift of God. The first was to have mind of the Passion of Christ. The second was a bodily sickness. The third, to have, of God's gift, three wounds.

For the first grace: it came to my mind with devotion. Methought I had great feeling for the Passion of Christ, but I desired to have yet more, by the grace of God. Methought I would like to have been that time with Mary Magdalen and others who were Christ's lovers, that I might have seen with bodily eyes the Passion of our Lord which he suffered for me, so that I might have suffered with Him as did others who loved Him. Notwithstanding the fact that I believed earnestly all the pains of Christ as Holy Church shews and teaches (and also the paintings of crucifixes made, by the grace of God, in conformity with the teaching of Holy Church, to the likeness of Christ's Passion as far as the skill of man may reach); notwithstanding all this true belief I desired a bodily sight, wherein I might have the more knowing of the bodily pains of our Lord, and Saviour, and of the compassion of our Lady and of all His true lovers who believed in His pains at that time and afterwards. For I would have been one of them and suffered along with them.

Other sight of God or shewing desired I never none until that my soul were gone forth from my body (for I trusted steadfastly that I should be saved). And this was my meaning: that I should afterwards, because of that shewing, have the more true mind in the Passion of Christ.

For the second grace: it came to my mind with contrition, freely, without any seeking—a wilful desire to have, of God's giving, a bodily sickness. I would that this bodily sickness might be grievous even to the point of death, so that I might in the sickness receive all the rites of Holy Church, I myself thinking that I should die; and I would that every creature that saw me might think the same. For I wished to have no comfort in fleshly or earthly living. In this sickness I desired to have all manner of pains, bodily and ghostly, such as I should have if I were to die: all the dreads, all the temptings of fiends, and all manner of their pains save of the out-passing of the soul; I hoped that it might be a speed to me when I should come to die, for I desired soon to be with my God.

These two desires—of the Passion and of the

sickness—I desired with a condition, as methought they passed the common course of prayers. Therefore I said: 'Lord, Thou knowest what I would have. If it be Thy will that I have it, grant it me; and if it be not Thy will, good Lord be not displeased, for I will not but as Thou willest.' The sickness desired I in my thoughts that I might have it when I was thirty years of age.

For the third grace: I heard a man of Holy Church tell the story of Saint Cecilia, in which telling I understood that she had received three wounds with a sword in the neck, from the which she pined to death. Moved by this I conceived a mighty desire, praying our Lord God that He would grant me three wounds during my lifetime, that is to say, the wound of contrition, the wound of compassion, and the wound of wilful longing for God. Right as I asked the other two graces with a condition, so I asked the third without any condition. These two desires aforesaid passed from my mind, and the third dwelt with me continually.

II

SICKNESS AND THE LAST RITES

And when I was thirty winters old and a half God sent me a bodily sickness, in the which I lay for three days and three nights. On the fourth night I received all the rites of Holy Church and thought not to be alive at daybreak. After this I languished for two days and two nights more, and on the third night I thought often times to have passed away and so too thought they who were about me. But in this I was right sorry and loath to die (though not for anything that was on earth that me liked to live for, nor for anything that I was afeared for; for I trusted in God). But it was because I would have lived on to have loved God better and for a longer time—that I might, by the grace of that living, have the more knowing and loving of God in the bliss of heaven, for methought all the time that I had lived here so little and so short in the regard of endless bliss. I thought thus: 'Good Lord, may my living be no longer to Thy worship?' And I was answered in my reason and by the feeling of my pains that I should die; and I assented fully, with all the will of my heart, to God's will.

Thus I endured till day and by then was my body dead from the middle downwards, as to feeling. Then was I moved to be set upright, leaning back, with cloths to my head, in order to have the more freedom of heart to be one with God's will, thinking on Him whilst my life would last.

They who were with me sent for the priest, my curate, to be at my ending. He came and a child with him, and brought a cross. By that time my eyes were set in my head and I could not speak. The priest set the cross before my face and said: 'Daughter, I have brought thee the image of thy Saviour. Look thereupon and comfort thee therewith in reverencing of Him who died for thee and me.' Methought that I was well as it was, for my eyes were set upwards, towards heaven whither I trusted to come. But nevertheless I assented to set my eyes upon the face of the crucifix if I could, to be able to endure the longer unto the time of mine ending. For methought I might longer endure to look straight forward than straight upward. After this my sight began to fail and it was all dark about me in the chamber, and murky as if it were night, except that on the image of the cross there remained the ordinary light. And, I knew not how, all that was beside the cross was as ugly to me as if it had been crowded with fiends.

After this the upper half of my body began to die as to feeling; my hands fell down on either side and also, from weakness, my head sank to one side. The most pain that I felt was shortness of breath and the failing of life. Then thought I truly that I was at the point of death.

And in this, suddenly all my pain was away from me: I was all whole as ever I was before or afterwards, and especially in the upper part of my body. I marvelled at this change, for methought it was a secret working of God and not of nature: yet, by the feeling of this ease I did not trust any the more that I should live, and the feeling of this ease was no true ease to me; for methought I had liefer been delivered of this world, and my heart was set thereon.

III

COMFORT AGAINST TEMPTATION

SUDDENLY it came to my mind that I should desire the second wound, of our Lord's gift and of His grace: that He would fill my body with mind and feeling of this blessed Passion, as I had before prayed. For I would that His pains were my pains, with compassion and then with longing for God. Thus methought that I might with His grace have His wounds that I had before desired. But in this I desired never of God either bodily sight or any manner of shewing, but compassion such as methought a kind soul might have towards our Lord Jesus, that for love willed to become a mortal man. With Him I desired to suffer whilst I lived in this mortal body, as God would give me grace.

In this, suddenly I saw the red blood trickle down from under the garland of thorns, all hot, freshly, plentifully, and lifelike, right as me thought that it was at that time when the garland of thorns was thrust on His blessed Head. Right so, both God and Man, the same suffered for me. I conceived truly and mightily that it was Himself that showed it me without any intermediary, and then I said: *Benedicite! Dominus.* This I said with reverence as my meaning, with a mighty voice. Full greatly I was astonished, for the wonder and marvel that I had, that He would be so homely with a sinful creature living in this wretched mortal life.

I took it thus, that for that time our Lord Jesus in His courteous love would shew me comfort before the time of my temptation—for methought it might be well that I should, by the sufferance of God and with His keeping, be tempted by fiends before I died—and with this sight of His blessed Passion, with the Godhead that I saw in my understanding, I saw that this was strength enough for me, yea, for all creatures living that should be saved, against all the fiends of hell and against all ghostly enemies.

IV

GOD: THE MAKER, THE LOVER, THE KEEPER

In this same time that I saw this bodily sight, our Lord shewed me a ghostly sight of His homely loving. I saw that He is to us all-thing that is good and comfortable for our help. He is our clothing, for love; He enwraps us and envelops us, embraces us and encloses us; He hovers over us, for tender love, that He may never leave us. And so in this sight I saw truly that He is everything that is good, as to mine understanding.

In this He shewed me a little thing, the quantity of a hazel nut, lying in the palm of my hand, and to my understanding it was as round as any ball. I looked thereupon and thought: 'What may this be?' And I was answered in a general way, thus: 'It is all that is made.' I marvelled how it could last, for methought it might fall suddenly to naught for littleness. And I was answered in my understanding: 'It lasts and ever shall last because God loves it, and so hath all-thing its being through the love of God.'

In this little thing I saw three parts. The first is that God made it; the second is that He loves it; the third is that God keeps it. But what is that to me? In sooth, the Maker, the Lover, the Keeper. For until I am substantially oned to Him I may never have love, rest, nor very bliss; that is to say, until I be so fastened unto Him that there be right naught that is made between my God and me. And who shall do this deed? In sooth, Himself, by His mercy and His grace, because He has made me for this and blessedfully restored me thereto.

In this, God brought our Lady to my understanding. I saw her ghostly, in bodily likeness, a simple maiden and meek, young of age, in the stature that she was when she conceived. Also God shewed me in part the wisdom and the truth of her soul, wherein I understood the reverent beholding where-with she beheld her God that is her Maker, marvelling with great reverence that He that was her Maker would be born of her. For this was her marvelling: that He that was her Maker would be born of her who was a simple creature of His making. And this wisdom of truth, this knowing the greatness of her Maker and the littleness of herself that is made, made her to say meekly to the Angel Gabriel: 'Lo me here, God's handmaiden!'[31] In this sight I saw truly that she is greater than all that God made beneath her in worthiness and in fulness of grace. For above her is nothing that is made but the blessed Manhood of Christ.

This little thing that is made, that is beneath our Lady, Saint Mary, God shewed it unto me as little as if it had been a hazel nut. Methought it might have fallen to nothing because of its littleness.

In this blessed revelation God shewed me three naughts, of which naughts this is the first that was shewed me; of this needs every man and woman who desires to live contemplatively to have knowing, that they should like to naught all things that are made for to have the love of God who is unmade. For this is the cause why they that are preoccupied wilfully with earthly business and ever more seek after worldly weal are not His in heart and in soul here: they love and seek their rest in this thing that is so little, wherein is no rest, and know not God who is All-Mighty, All-Wise and All-Good. For He is very rest.

God wills to be known and it pleaseth Him that we rest us in Him. For all that is beneath Him sufficeth not to us; and this is the cause why that no soul is rested until all that is made be as naught to him. When he is fully emptied, for love, to have Him who is all that is good, then is he able to receive ghostly rest.

V

GOD IS ALL THAT IS GOOD

IN that time that our Lord shewed this that I have now said, in ghostly sight, I saw the bodily sight—the plenteous bleeding of the Head—lasting. And as long as I saw that I said, often-times, *Benedicite! Dominus.*

In this first shewing of our Lord I saw six things in my understanding. The first is the tokens of His blissful Passion and the plenteous shedding of His Precious Blood. The second is the maiden—that she is His dearworthy Mother. The third is the blessed Godhead that ever was, and is, and ever shall be, All-Mighty, All-Wisdom and All-Love. The fourth is all-thing that He has made: it is great and fair and large and good; but the cause why it shewed so little to my sight was that I saw it in the presence of Him who is the Maker, 'for to a soul that sees the Maker of all things, all that is made seemeth full little'.[32] The fifth is that He has made all that is made, for love, and through the same love it is kept and ever shall be without end, as it is said before. The sixth is that God is all that is good, and the goodness that all these things have, is He. And all this our Lord shewed me in the first sight, and gave me space and time to behold it.

The bodily sight ceased and the ghostly sight remained in my understanding; I abided with reverent dread, rejoicing in what I saw and desiring as much as I durst for to see more if it were His will, or the same sight for a longer time.

VI

BEHOLD JESUS THAT IS TEACHER OF ALL

All that I say of myself I mean in the person of all my fellow-Christians, for I am learned in the ghostly shewing of our Lord that He means it thus. And therefore I pray you all for God's sake, and counsel you for your own profit, that ye leave the beholding of the wretched, worldly, sinful creature that it was shewed unto; and that ye mightily, wisely, lovingly and meekly behold God, that of His courteous love and of His endless goodness willed to shew generally this vision, in comfort of us all. And ye that hear and see this vision and this teaching, which is of Jesus Christ, to the edification of your souls, it is God's will and my desire that ye take it with as great joy and delight as if Jesus had shewn it to you as He did to me.

Because of the shewing I am not good, but only if I love God the better, and so may, and so should, each one do who sees it and hears it with good will and true intent. And so is my desire—that it should be for every such man the same profit as I desired for myself. Thereto was I moved by God the first time when I saw it, for since we are all one, the shewing is common to all. I am certain I saw it for the profit of many another, for in truth it was not shewed me that God loves me better than the least soul that is in grace; I am certain there are full many who never had shewing nor sight but of the common teaching of Holy Church and who love God better than I. For if I look at myself in particular I am right naught, but in general I am in oneness of charity with all my fellow-Christians; for in this oneness of charity standeth the life of all mankind that shall be saved.

For God is all that is good, and God has made all that is made and God loves all that He has made. So if any man or woman withdraw his love from any of his fellow-Christians, he loves right naught, for he loves not all; thus at that time he is not safe, for he is not in peace. He that loves his fellow-Christians in general, loves all that is. For in mankind that shall be saved is comprehended all that is, all that is made, and the Maker of all; for in man is God, and so in man is all. And he who thus in general loves all his fellow-Christians, he loves all; and he who thus loves he is safe. And thus I will to love and thus I love and thus I am safe (for I mean in the person of my fellow-Christian); and the more I love of this loving whilst I am here, the more I am like unto the bliss that I shall have in heaven without end, that is, God, who of His endless love would become our Brother and suffer for us.

I am certain that he that beholds it thus he shall be truly taught and mightily comforted if he needeth comfort. But God forbid that ye should say or take it thus, that I am a teacher, for I do not mean that, nor meant I ever so. For I am a woman, unlettered, feeble and frail. But I know well this that I say—I have it on the shewing of Him who is Sovereign Teacher—and truly charity urgeth me to tell you of it, for I would that God were known and my fellow-Christians helped (as I would be myself), to the more hating of sin and loving of God. Because I am a woman should I therefore believe that I ought not to tell you about the goodness of God since I saw at the same time that it is His will that it be known? And that shall ye see well in the same matter that follows after, if it be well and truly received. Then shall ye soon forget me that am a wretch, and act so that I hinder you not, and behold Jesus who is Teacher of all.

I speak of those who shall be saved, since at this time God shewed me none other. But in all things I believe as Holy Church teaches, for all things in this blessed shewing of our Lord I beheld as one with the teaching of Holy Church in God's sight; and never did I understand a thing therein (i.e. in the shewing) which harms me or withdraws me from the true teaching of Holy Church.

VII

WE ARE ALL ONE IN LOVE

ALL this blessed teaching of our Lord God was shewed to me in three parts, that is, by bodily sight, by words formed in my understanding, and by ghostly sight. The ghostly sight I may not nor cannot shew unto you as openly and as fully as I would, but I trust in our Lord God All-Mighty that He of his goodness and for your love shall make you take it more ghostly and more sweetly than I can or may tell it you; and so may it be, for we are all one in love!

In all this I was much stirred in charity to my fellow-Christians, that they might all see and know the same as I saw; and I would that it were a comfort to them all as it is to me. For this sight was shewed for my fellow-Christians in general and not just for me in particular. Of all that I saw, this was the most comfort to me: that our Lord is so homely and so courteous; and this most filled me with liking and security of soul.

Then said I to the folk that were with me: 'It is doomsday for me today.' This I said because I thought to have died, for that day on which a man or woman dies, he is judged as he shall be without end. I said this for I would they loved God more and set less store by the vanity of the world; and to make them have mind that this life is short, as they could see by me; for in all this time I thought to have died.

VIII

ALL-THING THAT IS DONE, IS DONE WELL

After this I saw with my bodily sight the Face of the crucifix that hung before me, in which I beheld continually a part of the Passion: contempt, spitting on, defiling of His body, buffeting His blessed Face and many languors and pains—more than I can tell; and oft changing of colour. At one time all His blessed Face was covered with dried blood. This I saw bodily, but dimly and darkly; and I desired more bodily light in order to have seen more clearly, and I was answered in my reason that if God willed to shew me more, He would, but that I needed no light but Him.

And after this I saw God in a point, that is, in my understanding, by which sight I saw that He is in all-thing. I gazed intently, perceiving and knowing in that sight that He does all that is done. I marvelled at this sight, with a soft dread, and thought, 'What is sin?' For I saw truly that God doth all thing, be it ever so little; nor is anything done by mere chance, but by the endless foresight of the wisdom of God; therefore it behoved me to grant that all-thing that is done is well done. And I was certain that God does no sin, therefore it seemed to me that sin is naught. For in all this sin was not shewed me. And I would no longer marvel at this but beheld our Lord and what He would shew me. In another time God shewed me what sin is, nakedly, by itself, as I shall tell afterwards.

And after this I saw, beholding, the body plenteously bleeding, hotly, freshly and in a lifelike way, just as I saw before in the head. This was shewed in the furrows of the scourging; the blood ran down so plenteously as to my sight, that methought it would have covered the bed and have spread all about if it had been so in reality for that time. God has made waters plenteous on earth for our service and for ease of our bodies, out of the tender love he has for us. Yet it pleaseth Him better that we betake us wholly to His Blessed Blood to wash us therewith from sin. For there is no drink that is made that He likes so well to give us—it is so plenteous and of our nature.

After this, ere God shewed me any wounds, He allowed me to behold longer both all that I had seen and all that was contained therein. And then, without voice or opening of lips this word was formed in my soul: 'Herewith is the fiend overcome.' This word said our Lord meaning His Passion, as He had shewn me before. In this our Lord brought unto my mind and shewed me a part of the fiend's malice and the whole of his unmight. Though He shewed me that His Passion is the overcoming of the fiend, God shewed that the fiend has now the same malice that he had before the Incarnation and as sorely he travails and as continually he sees that all chosen souls worshipfully escape him: that is all his sorrow. For all that God suffers him to do turns to our joy and to his pain and shame. And he has as great sorrow when God gives him leave to work as when he works not, and that because he may never do so great evil as he wills, for his might is all locked in God's hand. Also I saw our Lord scorning his malice and setting him at naught, and He wills that we do the same. At this sight I laughed mightily and that made those who were about me to laugh too, and their laughing was joy to me. I thought: 'I would that my fellow-Christians had seen what I saw, and then would they all have laughed with me.' But I saw not Christ laughing. Nevertheless it pleaseth Him that we laugh in comforting of ourselves and in joyfulness in God that the fiend is overcome.

After this I fell into a more serious mood and

said: 'I see! I see three things: game, scorn and earnest. I see game in that the fiend is overcome; I see scorn for that God scorns him and he shall be scorned; and I see earnest—that he is overcome by the Passion of our Lord Jesus Christ and by His death that was done full earnestly and with grievous travail.'

IX

GOD KEEPS US EVER ALIKE SECURE IN WEAL AND IN WOE

AFTER this our Lord said: 'I thank thee for thy service and for thy travail, and especially in thy youth.'

God shewed me three degrees of bliss that each soul shall have in heaven who willingly has served God in any degree on earth. The first degree is the worshipful thanking of our Lord God which he shall receive when he is delivered from pain. This thanking is so high and so worshipful that it will seem to him that it filleth him, though there were no other bliss. For methought that all the pain and travail that might be suffered by all men living could not have deserved the thanking that one man shall have who willingly has served his God.

For the second degree: all the blessed creatures that are in heaven shall see that worshipful thanking of our Lord God, and he maketh his service known to all who are in heaven.

And for the third: as new and as pleasing as it is received at that time so shall it last without end. I saw that goodly and sweetly was this said and shewed unto me, that the age of every man shall be known in heaven and rewarded for his willing service and for his time; and especially the age of those who wilfully and freely offer their youth unto God is surpassingly rewarded and wonderfully thanked.

After this our Lord shewed me a sovereign ghostly liking in my soul. In this liking I was filled with a sense of everlasting safety, mightily made secure without any dread. This feeling was so gladsome and so ghostly to me that I was in peace, in ease and in rest: there was nothing on earth that could have caused me grief. This lasted but a while and then I changed—I was left to myself in heaviness and weariness of myself and irksomeness of my life, so that I hardly had patience to live. There was no ease, no comfort, to my feeling, but hope, faith and charity; these I had in truth, but full little in feeling. And anon afterwards God gave me again the comfort and the rest in soul: liking and security so blissful and so mighty that no dread, nor sorrow, nor pain bodily or ghostly that could be suffered would have distressed me. And then the pain appeared again, to my feeling, and again the joy and the liking, then the one and now the other, divers times (I should say about twenty times). And in the time of joy I might have said with Paul: 'Nothing shall separate me from the charity of Christ.' And in pain I might have said with Saint Peter: 'Lord, save me, I perish!'[33]

This vision was shewed me to teach me (as to my understanding of it) that it is needful to every man to feel in this wise—sometimes to be in comfort and sometimes to fail and be left to himself. God wills that we know that He keeps us ever alike secure in weal and in woe and loves us as much in woe as in weal. And sometimes for the profit of his soul a man is left to himself even if sin is not the cause; for in this time I sinned not, wherefor I should be left to myself. Nor did I deserve to have the blissful feeling. But freely God gives weal when it pleaseth Him and suffers us to be in woe sometime, and both is of love. For it is God's will that we hold us in comfort with all our might; for bliss is lasting, without end, whereas pain is passing and shall be brought to naught.

Therefore it is not God's will that we follow the feelings of pain in sorrowing and mourning for them, but that we at once pass them over and hold us in endless liking of God All-Mighty that is our Lover and Keeper.

X

A PART OF HIS PASSION

After this Christ shewed me a part of His Passion, near His dying: I saw that sweet Face as it were dry and bloodless with the paleness of death, then turning more deathly pale, languishing, and change to a bluish colour, the colour of death, which grew deeper as the flesh became more deathlike. For all the pains that Christ suffered in His body shewed in the blessed Face (as far as I could see), and especially in the lips; there I saw these four colours, in those lips that I had seen before fresh and ruddy, lifelike and pleasant to my sight. This was a heavy change to see, this deep pallor of dying. The nostrils also changed and dried up, to my sight. This pining seemed to me as long as if He had been a seven-night on the point of death, always suffering pain.

And methought the drying of Christ's flesh was the greatest pain of the Passion—and the last. In this drying was brought to my mind this word that Christ said: 'I thirst.'[34] For I saw in Christ a double thirst: one bodily, another ghostly; this word was shewed to me for the bodily thirst. And as for the ghostly thirst—it was shewed to me after the manner in which I shall say afterwards.

I understood for the bodily thirst that which the body suffered from failing of moisture, for the blessed flesh and bones were wholly drained of blood and moisture. For a long, long time the blessed body was bleeding dry from the tearing wounds of the nails, caused by the heaviness of the head and the weight of the body. The wind blowing without dried Him too, and the cold tortured Him more than all other pains—more than my heart can think of. Such pains I saw that all is too little that I can tell or say of them, for it may not be told, unless every soul should feel in himself that which was in Christ Jesus, according to the saying of Saint Paul: 'Let that mind be in you which was in Christ Jesus.'[35] For though he suffered but once, as I know well, yet He wished to shew it me and fill me with mind of His Passion, as I had before desired.

My mother, who stood, with others, and beheld me, lifted up her hand to my face to lock my eyes, for she thought that I was about to die or else that I had just died; and this much increased my sorrow. For notwithstanding all my pains I would not have been hindered (i.e. from looking at our Lord) for the love that I had in Him. And moreover, in all this time of Christ's presence I felt no pain but for Christ's pains. Then methought I knew fully for what pain it was that I asked, for methought that my pains surpassed those of any bodily death. I thought: 'Is any pain in hell like this pain?' And I was answered in my reason that despair is greater, for that is ghostly pain; but of bodily pain none is greater than this. How might my pain be greater than to see Him suffer that is all my life, all my bliss and all my joy?

Here felt I truly that I loved Christ so much above myself that methought it had been a great ease to me to have died bodily. Herein I saw a part of the compassion of our Lady, Saint Mary, for Christ and she were so oned in love that the greatness of her love was the cause of the greatness of her pain. For in so much as she loved Him more than all others her pain surpassed all others' pain; and so all His disciples and all His true lovers suffered pains greater than those of their own bodily dying. For I am sure, by mine own feeling, that the least of them loved Him more than they loved themselves; here I saw a great oneing between Christ and us, for when He was in pain we were in pain: all creatures that might suffer pain suffered with Him, and they who knew Him not had this for their pain, that all creatures, sun and moon, withdrew their service—and so were they all left in sorrow for the time. Thus they that loved Him suffered pain because of their love, and they that loved Him not suffered pain because of the failing of comfort of all creatures.

During this time I would have looked aside from the cross but I dared not. For I knew well that while I looked upon the cross I was safe and sound. Therefore I would not consent to put my soul in peril, for away from the cross nothing was certain except the terrors of the fiend. Then came the thought to my mind, as if the words had been said to me in a friendly way: 'Look up to heaven, to His Father!' Then saw I well, with the faith that I felt, that since there was nothing between the cross and heaven that might have distressed me, it behoved me either to look up or else to answer. I answered and I said: 'I may not—for thou art my heaven.' This I said because I would not—for I had rather be in that pain until doomsday than have come to heaven otherwise than by Him. For I knew well that He who bought me at so sore a cost would release me when He willed.

XI

LOVE WAS WITHOUT BEGINNING

Thus chose I Jesus for my heaven, whom I saw only in pain at that time. Me liked no other heaven than Jesus, who shall be my bliss when I am there. And this has ever been a comfort to me: that I chose Jesus for my heaven in all this time of passion and of sorrow; and it has been a learning to me, that I should evermore do so, and choose only Him for my heaven in weal and in woe.

Thus saw I my Lord Jesus languishing for a long time, for the oneing of the Godhead, for love, to the manhood gave Him strength to suffer more than all men might suffer. I mean not alone more pain than all men might suffer, but also that He suffered more anguish than all men that ever were, from the first beginning to the last day. No tongue may tell, no heart fully think of the suffering that our Saviour endured for us, having regard to the worthiness of this highest, worshipful King, and to His shameful despites and painful death. For He who was highest and worthiest was most completely despoiled and most utterly humiliated. But the love that made Him suffer all this—it passes as far all His pains as heaven is above earth. For the passion was a deed done in time by the working of love; but the love was without beginning, and is, and ever shall be, without any end.

Suddenly, while I was still beholding the same cross He changed to a blissful expression of countenance. The changing of His expression changed mine, and I was as glad and merry as it was possible to be. Then brought our Lord merrily to my mind: 'Where is now[36] any point of thy pain or of thy grief?' And I was full merry.

XII

'IF I MIGHT SUFFER MORE, I WOULD SUFFER MORE'

THEN said our Lord, asking: 'Art thou well content that I suffered for thee?' 'Yea, good Lord,' said I. 'Gramercy, good Lord: blessed mayest Thou be!' 'If thou be content,' said our Lord, 'I am content. It is a joy, and a bliss and an endless liking to me that ever I suffered Passion for thee; for if I might suffer more, I would suffer more.'

In this feeling mine understanding was lifted up into heaven, and there I saw three heavens, of which sight I was greatly marvelled and thought: 'I saw three heavens and all in the blessed manhood of Christ; and none is more, none is less, none is higher, none is lower, but all are alike equal in bliss.'

For the first heaven Christ shewed me his Father—in no bodily likeness but in His property and in His liking. The working of the Father it is this: that He gives meed to His Son Jesus Christ. This gift and this meed is so blissful to Jesus, that the Father might have given no meed that might have pleased Him better. For the first heaven—that is the rejoicing of the Father showed to me as a heaven—it was full blissful. For He is full blessed in all the deeds that He has done about our salvation, whereby we are not only His through the redemption, but also by the courteous gift of His Father. We are His bliss. We are His meed. We are His worship. We are His crown. This that I say is such great bliss to Jesus that He sets at naught His travail and His hard Passion and cruel and shameful death.

And in these words, 'If I might suffer more, I would suffer more'—I saw truly that if He might die as often as once for every soul who shall be saved, as He died once for all, love should never let Him have rest until He had done it. And when he had done it, He would set it at naught out of love; for all this is to Him but little seen in the light of His love.

That shewed He me well earnestly, saying this word: 'If I might suffer more—' He said not 'If it were needful to suffer more', for though it be not needful and He could suffer more, He would suffer more. This deed and this work about our salvation was planned as well as He might plan it; it was carried out as worshipfully as Christ might do it. In this I saw a fullness of bliss in Christ; but this bliss would not have been complete if the work of our salvation could any better have been done than it was done.

And in these three words—'It is a joy, a bliss and an endless liking to me'—were shewed three heavens, as thus: For the joy I understood the good-pleasure of the Father; for the bliss, the worship of the Son; and for the endless liking, the Holy Ghost. The Father is pleased. The Son is worshipped. The Holy Ghost is satisfied.

Jesus wills that we pay heed to this joy that is in the blessed Trinity for our salvation, and that we rejoice as much, with His grace, while we are here. This was shewed me in this word: Art thou well content?' By that other word that Christ said: 'if thou be content, I am content', He shewed me the understanding as if He had said: 'That is joy and liking enough for me, and I ask naught else for my travail, but that I might please thee.'

Plenteously and fully was this shewed me. Think also wisely of the greatness of this word—'That ever I suffered Passion for thee'—for in that word was a high knowing of the love and liking that He had in our salvation.

XIII

'LO, HOW I LOVED THEE!'

FULL merrily and gladly our Lord looked into His side, and beheld and said this word: 'Lo, how I loved thee!', as if he had said: 'My child, if you cannot look on my Godhead, see here how I allowed my side to be opened and my heart cloven in two, so that all the blood and water that was therein poured out. And this gives me joy and so will I that it do to thee.' This our Lord shewed me to make us glad and merry.

With the same gladness He looked down at His right-hand side and brought to my mind where our Lady stood in the time of His Passion and said: 'Wilt thou see her?' And I answered and said: 'Yea, good Lord, gramercy, if it be Thy will.' Oft times I had prayed for it and thought to have seen her in bodily likeness. But I saw her not thus. And Jesus, when He said this word, shewed me a ghostly sight of her: just as I had before seen her little and simple, right as He shewed her then high and noble and glorious, and pleasing to Him above all creatures. Thus He wills that it be known that all those who like in Him should like in her, and in the liking that He has in her, and she in Him. And in that word: 'Wilt thou see her?' methought I had the greatest liking that He could have given me, with the ghostly shewing that He gave me of her. For our Lord granted me no special shewing but that of our Lady, Saint Mary, and her He shewed me three times: The first time was at the moment of her conceiving Him; the second time, as she was in her sorrow under the cross; and the third time, as she is now—in liking, worship and joy.

After this our Lord shewed Himself to me more glorified, as to my sight, than I saw Him before and in this shewing was I taught that every contemplative soul to whom it is given to behold and feel God, shall see her and pass unto God by contemplation.

And after this teaching—homely, courteous and blissful and very life—oft times our Lord Jesus said to me: 'I it am that is highest. I it am that thou lovest. I it am that thou likest. I it am that thou servest. I it am that thou longest for. I it am that thou desirest. I it am that thou hast in mind. I it am that is all. I it am that Holy Church teaches and preaches to thee. I it am that shewed myself to thee before.'

These words I reveal but only so that each man, according to the grace of understanding and loving that God gives him, may receive them in the way our Lord means him to.

Afterwards our Lord brought unto my mind the longing that I had for Him before, and I saw that nothing hindered me but sin—and so, I beheld, was it generally in us all. And methought: 'If sin had not been we should all have been clean and like to our Lord—as He made us.' And thus in my folly at this time often I wondered why sin was not hindered by the great foreseeing wisdom of God, 'for then', methought, '*all* should have been well!' This feeling was much to be despised, yet mourning and sorrow I made because of it, without reason or discretion, out of full great pride.

Nevertheless Jesus, in this vision, informed me of all that I needed to know. (I say not that I need no more teaching, for our Lord, with the shewing of this, has left me to Holy Church: I am hungry and thirsty, and needy and sinful and frail, and wilfully submit myself to the teaching of Holy Church, with all my fellow-Christians, unto the end of my life.)

Jesus answered by this word and said: 'Sin must needs be.' In this word *sin*, our Lord brought to my mind, in general, all that is not good: the shameful despite and the utter naughting that He bore for us in this life, and in His dying, and all the pains and passions of all His creatures, ghostly and bodily. (For we are all partly naughted, and we should be, following our Master Jesus until we be fully purified. That is to say, until we have fully mortified our own deadly flesh and those of our inward affections which are not good.) And the beholding of this, with all the pains that ever were or ever shall be, was shewed me in an instant, and swiftly passed over into comfort. For our good Lord would not that the soul be afeard of this ugly sight.

But I saw not sin, for I know by faith it has no manner of substance nor part of being, and it could not be known except by the pain that it is the cause of. And this pain—it is something that has being, as to my sight, while it lasts, for it purifies us and makes us to know ourselves and ask mercy. For the Passion of our Lord is comfort to us against all this, and so is His blessed will unto all that shall be saved. He comforts readily and sweetly by His words and says: 'But all shall be well, and all manner of thing shall be well.' These words were shewed full tenderly, shewing no more of blame towards me nor to anyone that shall be saved. Then were it a great unkindness for me to blame or wonder at God because of my sins, since He blames not me for sinning.

Thus I saw how Christ has compassion on

us because of sin; and right as I was before, with the Passion of Christ, filled full of pain and compassion, just so in this I was in part filled with compassion for all my fellow-Christians. And then saw I that when compassion for his fellow-Christians flows naturally from a man who is in charity, this is Christ in him.

XIV

WE SHOULD ENJOY ONLY IN OUR BLESSED SAVIOUR, JESUS

But on this ye shall ponder, beholding this state of things sorrowfully and with mourning, saying thus to our Lord in my meaning, with full great dread: 'Ah, good Lord, how might all be well, in view of the great harm that is come by sin to Thy creatures?' And I desired, as much as I dared, to have some more open declaration wherewith I might be eased in this matter. And to this our blessed Lord answered full meekly, and with full lovely cheer. He shewed me that Adam's sin was the greatest harm that ever was done or ever shall be done, unto the world's end; and also He shewed me that this is openly known in all Holy Church on earth. Furthermore He taught me that I should behold the glorious reparation. For this making of reparation is more pleasing to the blessed Godhead, and more worshipful to man's salvation

—there is no comparison—than ever was the sin of Adam harmful.

What our blessed Lord means, then, is that we should take heed of His teaching: 'For since I have made well the greatest harm, it is my will that thou know thereby that I shall make well all that is less.'

He gave me understanding about two parts of this word. The one part is our Saviour and our salvation. This blessed part is open and clear, and fair and light and plenteous, for all mankind that is of good will or that shall be, is comprehended in this part. To this are we bidden by God, and drawn and counselled and taught—inwardly by the Holy Ghost and outwardly by Holy Church—by the same grace. In this our Lord wills that we be occupied, having our enjoyment in Him; for He enjoys in us. And the more plenteously that we take of this, with reverence and meekness, the more we deserve thanks from Him, and the more we benefit ourselves. Thus may we say, enjoying: 'Our part is our Lord.'

The other part is shut off from us, and hidden; that is to say, all that is outside of our salvation. For this is our Lord's privy counsels. It belongs to the royal lordship of God for to have His privy counsels in peace, and it belongs to His servants, out of obedience and reverence, not to will to know His counsels.

Our Lord has pity and compassion on us because some creatures make themselves so busy about this, and I am certain if we know how much we should please Him and ease ourselves by not doing it, we would leave off doing it. The saints in heaven will to know nothing except what our Lord wills to shew them; also, their charity and their desire is regulated according to the will of our Lord. And thus ought we to will, and not want to be like to Him; and then shall we nothing will or desire but the will of our Lord as He does (for we are all one in God's meaning).

Here was I taught that we should enjoy only in our blessed Saviour, Jesus, and trust in Him for all thing.

XV

GOD HATH RUTH AND COMPASSION ON US

And thus our good Lord answered to all the questions and doubts that I might make, saying full comfortably in this wise: 'I will make all things well. I shall make all things well. I may make all things well, and I can make all things well; and thou shalt see thyself that all things shall be well.'

Where He says He *may*, I understand for the Father. And where He says He *can*, I understand for the Son. And where He says *I will*, I understand for the Holy Ghost. And where He says *I shall*, I understand for the unity of the Blessed Trinity: three Persons in one truth. And where He says *thou shalt see thyself*, I understand the oneing of all mankind that shall be saved, into the blissful Trinity.

In these five words God willeth that we be enclosed in rest and in peace; and thus has the ghostly thirst of Christ an end. For this is the ghostly thirst—the love-longing—and that lasts and ever shall until we see that sight on doomsday. For we who shall be saved and shall be Christ's joy and His bliss are still here below, and shall be, until that day. Therefore this is the thirst: the failing of His bliss, in that He has us not in Him as wholly as He shall then have.

All this was shewed me in the shewing of compassion (for that thirst shall cease on doomsday). Thus He hath ruth and compassion on us; and He has a longing to have us. But His wisdom and His love permit not the end to come until the best time.

And in these same five words before said: 'I may make all things well etc.', I understand a mighty comfort that shall be in all the words of our Lord that are yet to come. For just as the Blessed Trinity made all things out of nothing, right so the same Blessed Trinity shall make well all that is not well. It is God's will that we have great regard for all the deeds that He has done, for He will that we know thereby all that He shall do. And that shewed He me in this word that He said: 'And thou shalt see thyself that all manner of thing shall be well.' This I understand in two manners: one I am well content that I know it not; the other I am glad and merry because I shall know it.

It is God's will that we know that all shall

be well in general, but it is not God's will that we should know it now except as it belongs to us for the time; and that is the teaching of Holy Church.

XVI

A COMFORT AGAINST SIN

GOD shewed me the full great pleasure that He has in all men and women who mightily and meekly and worshipfully receive the preaching and teaching of Holy Church. For He is Holy Church. He is the Ground; He is the Substance. He is the Teaching; He is the Teacher. He is the End. He is the Centre towards which every true soul is striving; and He is known, and shall be known, to each soul to whom the Holy Ghost declares it.

And I am certain that all those who seek in this way shall succeed, for they seek God.

All this that I have now said, and more that I shall say afterwards, is a comfort against sin. For first when I saw that God does all that is done, I saw not sin, and then saw I that all is well. But when God shewed me sin, then said He 'all shall be well'.

And when God Almighty had shewed me plenteously and fully of His goodness, I desired concerning a certain person that I love , how it should be with her. In such desire I hindered myself, and I was not enlightened on this occasion. But I was answered in my reason, as it were by a friendly man: 'Take it in general, and behold the courtesy of thy Lord God as He shews it to thee. For it is more worship to God to behold Him in all, than in any special thing.' I assented, and with that I learnt that it is more worship to God to know all things in general, than to take pleasure in any particular thing. And if I should act wisely, in accordance with this teaching, I should not be glad for any special thing nor distressed by any manner of thing; for '*all* shall be well'.

God brought to my mind that I should sin, and for the liking that I had in beholding of Him I attended not readily to that shewing, and our Lord full courteously waited until I would attend. Then our Lord brought to my mind, with my sins, the sin of all my fellow-Christians: all in a general way and nothing in special.

XVII

'I KEEP THEE FULL SURELY'

ALTHOUGH our Lord shewed me that I should sin, by me alone I understand all men. At this I conceived a soft dread, and to this our Lord answered me thus: 'I keep thee full surely.' This word was said to me with more love and sureness of ghostly keeping than I can or may tell. For, as it was before shewed to me that I should sin, right so was the comfort shewed to me: sureness of keeping for all my fellow-Christians.

What may make me more to love my fellow-Christians than to see in God that He loves all that shall be saved as if it were all one soul?

And in every soul that shall be saved there is a goodly will that never assented to sin, nor ever shall. For as there is a beastly will in man's lower nature that may will no good, so is there a goodly will in the higher part of man that ever wills good, and that may no more will evil than the Persons of the Blessed Trinity.

And this shewed our Lord to me, in the wholeness of love that we stand in, in His sight —yea, that He loves us now as well while we are here, as He shall do when we are there before His blessed Face.

Also, God shewed me that sin is no shame, but worship, to man. For in this sight mine understanding was lifted up into heaven, and then came truly to my mind David, Peter and Paul, Thomas of India and the Magdalen: how they are known in the Church on earth with their sins, to their worship. And as it is to them no shame that they have sinned, no more is it in the bliss of heaven. For there the tokening of sin is turned into worship. Right so our Lord God shewed me them as examples of all others that shall come thither.

Sin is the sharpest scourge that any chosen soul may be beaten with: which scourge thoroughly bruises and breaks men and women and makes them seem naught in their own sight, so far forth that it seems to them as if they are not worthy but as it were to sink into hell. But when contrition takes a man, by the touching of the Holy Ghost, then is his bitterness turned into hope of God's mercy. Then begin his wounds to heal and the soul to quicken, since he has turned unto the life of Holy Church. The Holy Ghost leads him to confession, wilfully to show his sins, nakedly and truly and with great sorrow and shame that he has so defaced the fair image of God. Then he receives penance for each sin, as enjoined by his confessor who is grounded in the teaching of Holy Church by the Holy Ghost. By this medicine it behoves every sinful soul to be healed, and especially of sins that are mortal in themselves. Though he be healed, his wounds are still seen before God though not as wounds but as tokens of worship. And so, contrarywise, as sin is punished here with sorrow and with penance, it shall be rewarded in heaven by the courteous love of our Lord God Almighty, who wills that none who comes thither shall lose his labour. The reward that we shall receive there shall not be little—it shall be high, glorious and worshipful; and so shall all shame turn into worship and into more joy. And I am certain, by mine own feeling, that the more each loving soul sees this in the kind and courteous love of God, the more loath is he to sin.

XVIII

ALL THINGS ARE GOOD EXCEPT SIN

But now if thou be moved to say or think: 'Since this is true, then were it a good thing to sin, so as to have the more reward', beware of this stirring, and despise it, for it is of the enemy. For the soul that wilfully receives this suggestion may never be safe until he be amended, even as from mortal sin. For if all the pain that is in hell and in purgatory and on earth, death and other pains and sin, were laid before me, I had rather choose all that pain than sin. For sin is so vile, and so much to be hated, that it may be likened to no pain, which pain is not sin; for all things are good except sin, and nothing is wicked except sin. Sin is neither an act nor an affection, and when a soul wilfully chooses sin, that is pain as for his God, in the end he has right naught.

That pain seems to me the most severe of hell's pains, because he has not his God; for in all pains a soul may have God, except in the pain of sin.

And as mighty and as wise as God is for to save man, as willing is He. For Christ Himself is the foundation of all the laws of Christian men, and He has taught us to do good for evil. Here may we see that He is Himself this charity and does unto us as He teaches us to do, for He wills that we be like unto Him in onehead of endless love to ourselves and to our fellow-Christians: no more than His love for us is broken because of our sins, no more will He that our love for ourselves or for our fellow-Christians be broken. But let us nakedly hate sin, and endlessly love the soul as God loves it; for this word that God said, that He keeps us full surely, is an endless comfort.

XIX

CONCERNING PRAYER

AFTER this, our Lord shewed me concerning prayer. I saw two conditions on the part of those who pray, according to that which I have felt in myself. One is, that they will pray for nothing at all except what is God's will and to His worship. The other is that they set themselves mightily and continually to beseech that thing that is God's will and to His worship: and that is how I have understood it from the teaching of Holy Church. For in this shewing our Lord taught me the same, to pray to have, of God's gift, Faith, Hope and Charity, and to keep us therein unto the end of our lives.

And unto this end we say: *Pater Noster*, *Ave* and *Credo*, with such devotion as God will give. Thus we pray for all our fellow-Christians and for all manner of men; for God's will is that we desire for all manner of men and women the same virtue and grace that we ought to desire for ourselves.

But yet in all this, oft-times our trust is not full; for we are not full sure that God Almighty hears us, because of our unworthiness, as it seems to us, and because we feel right naught. For we are as barren and as dry, often, after our prayers as we were before, and this in respect of our feeling. It is this folly of ours which is the cause of our weakness, as I have myself experienced.

And all this our Lord brought suddenly to my mind and mightily and in a life-like manner strengthening me against this manner of weakness in prayer, said: 'I am the ground of thy beseeching. First, it is my will that thou have it. Then I make thee to will it. And then I make thee beseech it. And if thou beseechest it how should it then be that thou shouldest not have thy beseeching?' And thus, in the first reason, with the three that follow afterwards, our Lord showed a mighty comfort.

In the first reason, where He says: 'If thou beseechest'—there He shews His own full great pleasure and the endless reward that He will give us for our beseeching. And in the fourth reason, where He says: 'How should it then be that thou shouldst not have thy beseeching?', there He gives a firm undertaking that He will hear our prayers (for we trust not as mightily as we should).

Our Lord wills that we both pray and trust

in this way. For the purpose of the reasons beforesaid is to make us mighty against weakness in our prayers. For it is God's will that we pray, and to this He stirs us in these words aforesaid. For He willeth that we be full sure that our prayer shall be answered; because prayer pleases God. Prayer puts man at peace with himself, and makes him serene and meek who was before in strife and travail. Prayer ones the soul to God. For though the soul be ever like to God in kind and in substance, it is often unlike in condition, through sin on man's part. Prayer, then, makes the soul like to God in condition as it is in kind, hence He teaches us to pray and mightily to trust that we shall have what we pray for. All thing that is done would be done though we never prayed for it; but the love of God is so great that He holds us as partners in His good deeds, and therefore He stirs us to pray for that which it pleases Him to do. For whatever prayer or good will that we have, of His gift, He will reward us endlessly —and this was shewed me in this word: 'If thou beseech it.'

In this word God shewed me His great pleasure and His great liking, as if He were much beholden to us for every good deed that we do (although it is He who does it), and because we beseech Him earnestly to do that thing that is pleasing to Him. As if He said:

'In what way mightest thou please me more than to beseech me earnestly, wisely and wilfully to do that thing that I will to do?'

In this way prayer brings about the union between God and man's soul. For what time that man's soul is homely with God, him needeth not to pray, but to behold reverently what He says: for in all the time that this was shewed me I was not stirred to pray, but to have always this in my mind, for comfort, that, when we see God, we have that which we desire, and then us needeth not to pray. But when we see not God, then it needeth us to pray because of our failing, and to put ourselves in contact with Jesus. For when a soul is tempted, troubled by unrest and left to itself, then it is time to pray and to make himself simple and supple to God. Unless he be supple, no manner of prayer makes God supple towards him.

For God is ever the same in love, but during the time when man is in sin he is so unmighty, so unwise and so unloving, that he can love neither God nor himself. The greatest defect that he has, is blindness, for he sees not all this. Then the holy love of God All-Mighty, that ever is one, gives him a sight of himself. At this he thinks that God is angry with him because of his sins, and then is he stirred to contrition, and by confession and other good deeds to slake the wrath of God, until he finds peace of soul and delicacy of conscience. It seems to him now that God has forgiven his sins, and this is true. The soul is made aware that God is turned to behold it, as if it had been in pain or in prison, saying thus: 'I am glad that thou art come to rest; for I have ever loved thee and love thee, and now thou lovest me.'

And thus with prayers (as I have before said), and with other good works that are customary, according to the teaching of Holy Church, is the soul oned to God.[37]

XX

'THOU SHALT BE FULFILLED WITH JOY AND BLISS'

BEFORE this time I had often great longing, of God's gift, to be delivered from this world and from this life, because I would be with my God in bliss where I hope firmly, through his mercy, to be without end. For oft times I beheld the woe that is here and the weal and the blessed being there; and if there had been no pain on earth but the absence of our Lord God, methought sometimes it were more than I could bear. And this made me to mourn and earnestly to long. Then God said to me concerning patience and endurance, thus: 'Suddenly thou shalt be taken from all thy pain, from all thy distress, and from all thy woe; and thou shalt come up above, and thou shalt have me for thy reward. Thou shalt be filled full of joy and bliss and thou shalt have no manner of sickness, no manner of misliking, no weakness of will—but ever joy and bliss without end. Why should it then grieve thee to suffer for a while, since it is my will and my worship?'

Also in this reason: 'Suddenly thou shalt be taken', I saw how God rewards man for the patience that he has in abiding God's will in his time of pilgrimage, and how man lengthens his patience over the time of his living because he knows not the time of his passing. This is a great profit. For if a man knew his time, he would not have patience throughout that time. Also, God wills that while the soul is in the body, it should seem to itself that it is ever on the point of being taken. For all this life, in this languor that we have here, is but a point. And when we are taken suddenly out of pain into bliss it shall be naught, and therefore said our Lord: 'Why should it then grieve thee to suffer for a while, since it is my will and my worship?'

It is God's will that we take His behests and His comfortings as largely and as mightily as we may take them; and also He wills that we take our abiding and our distress as lightly as we may take them, and set them at naught. For the more lightly that we take them, the less price we set on them, for love, the less pain shall we have in the feeling of them and the more thanks shall we have for them.

In this blessed revelation I was truly taught that whatever man or woman wilfully keeps choosing God during his life, may be sure that he is chosen. Keep this truly, for truly it is God's will that we be as sure, in trust, of the bliss of heaven while we are here, as we shall be in certainty when we are there. And ever the more liking and joy we take in this sureness, with reverence and meekness, the better it liketh Him. For I am sure if there had been none but I that should be saved, God would have done all that He has done, for me. And so should each soul think, in knowing of his lover, forgetting, if he can, all creatures, and thinking that God has done for him all that he has done. And this, it seems to me, should stir a soul for to love and like Him and naught dread except Him. For it is His will that we know that all the might of our enemy is locked in our Friend's hand, and therefore a soul that knows this surely, shall naught dread but Him that he loves, and shall reckon all other dreads among passions, and bodily sickness, and imaginations.

Therefore if a man be in so much pain, in so much woe, and in so much distress that it seems to him that he can think of right naught except of the pain he is in, or the distress which he feels—as soon as he may let him pass lightly over it and set it at naught. And why? Because God will be known: for if we knew Him and loved Him we would have patience and be in great rest, and all that He does would be pleasing to us. This our Lord shewed me in these words that He said: 'Why should it then grieve thee to suffer a while, since it is my will and my worship?'

XXI

'WRETCH THAT I AM!'

SOON after this, I came to myself and returned to my bodily sickness, understanding that I should live. And as a wretch I heaved and moaned over the bodily pains that I felt, and thought it great irksomeness that I should longer live. I was as barren and dry as if I had had but little comfort before, because of falling again into pain, and for failing of ghostly feeling.

Then came a religious person to me and asked me hôw I fared. And I said that I had raved that day, and he laughed loud and heartily. I said: 'The cross that stood at my bed's foot it bled fast.' And with this word, the person that I spoke to became all serious, marvelling. And anon I was sore ashamed of my recklessness and I thought thus: 'This man takes seriously the least word that I might say, since he says nothing thereto.' And when I saw that he took it in this way and with such great reverence, I became right greatly ashamed and would have been shriven. But I could tell it to no priest, for I thought 'How should a priest believe me? I believed not our Lord God.' At the time when I saw Him I believed it firmly, and it was then my will and my meaning to continue to believe without end. But as a fool I allowed it to pass from my mind, wretch that I am. This was a great sin, a great want of filial love, that I, out of vexation at feeling bodily pain, so unwisely left aside for the time the comfort of all this blessed shewing of our Lord.

Here may you see what I am of myself. But herein would not our courteous Lord leave me. I lay until night, trusting in His mercy, and then I began to sleep.

In my sleep, at the beginning, methought the fiend seized me by the throat and would have strangled me; but he could not. Scarcely alive, I woke out of my sleep. The persons who were with me saw this, and bathed my temples; and my heart began to take comfort. Soon a little smoke came in at the door, with a great heat and a foul stench. I said: '*Benedicite! Dominus*—Is everything here on fire?' And I thought it was a bodily fire that would burn us to death. I asked them that were with me if they noticed any stench; they said no, they noticed nothing. I said: 'Blessed be God!' for then knew I well that it was the fiend which was come to tempest me; and once more I received that which our Lord had shewed me that same day with all the faith of Holy Church (for I hold both as one), and fled thereto as to my comfort. And very soon all vanished away and I was brought to great rest and peace, without sickness of body or dread of conscience.

XXII

IN US IS HIS HOMELIEST HOME

THEN I remained still, awake; and our Lord opened my ghostly eyes and shewed me my soul in the midst of my heart. I saw my soul as large as if it were a kingdom, and from what I saw therein, methought it was a worshipful City. In the midst of this City is seated our Lord, true God and true man—beautiful in person and tall of stature—the worshipful, highest Lord; and I saw Him in majesty covered with glory. He sits in the very centre of the soul, in peace and rest, and rules and cares for heaven and earth and all that is. The Manhood, with the Godhead, sits in rest, and the Godhead rules and directs without any instrument or busy-ness; and my soul is blessedfully possessed by the Godhead that is Sovereign Might, Sovereign Wisdom, Sovereign Goodness.

The place that Jesus takes in our soul He shall never leave, without end; for in us is His homeliest home and the most pleasing to Him to dwell in.

This was a delectable sight, and a restful one, since it is so in truth without end. And the beholding of this while we are here is full pleasing to God and full great profit to us: the soul that thus beholds, this sight makes like to Him that is beheld and ones it in rest and in peace. And this was a singular joy and a bliss to me, that I saw Him *sit*, for the beholding of this sitting shewed to me sureness of His endless dwelling. And I knew truly that it was He that shewed me all before.

When I had beheld this with full attentiveness, then our Lord shewed me words, full meekly, without voice and without opening of lips, as He had done before, and said full soberly: 'Know it well: it was no raving that thou saw today. But take it and believe it, and keep thee thereto, and thou shalt not be overcome.'

These last words were said to me for learning of full true sureness that it is our Lord Jesus who shewed me all. For right as in the first word that our Lord shewed me, meaning His blessed Passion: 'Herewith is the fiend overcome'—right so He said in the last word, with full true sureness: 'Thou shalt not be overcome.' And this learning and this true comfort, it is for all my fellow-Christians in general, as I have before said; such is God's will. This word: 'Thou shalt not be overcome,' was said full clearly and full mightily, for sureness and comfort against all tribulations that may come. He said not: 'Thou shalt not be tempested; thou shalt not be travailed; thou shalt not be distressed.' But He said: 'Thou shalt not be *overcome*.'

God wills that we pay heed to His word and that we be ever mighty in sureness, in weal and in woe. For He loves us and likes us, and so wills He that we love Him and like Him—and mightily trust in Him. 'And all shall be well.'

Soon afterwards, all was ended and I saw no more.

XXIII

EVER HE LONGS TO HAVE OUR LOVE

After this the fiend came again with his heat and with his stench, and made me full restless—the stench was so vile and so painful, and the bodily heat so dreadful and oppressive. Also I heard a bodily jangling and speaking as if it had been of two people (and both, to my thinking, jangled at once, with great earnestness, as though they were holding a parliament); all was soft muttering, and I understood not what they said. And all this was to stir me to despair, as methought, but I trusted earnestly in God and comforted myself with bodily speech, as I would have done any other person that had been so travailed.

Methought this busy-ness might be likened to no bodily busy-ness. My bodily eyes I fixed upon the same cross that I had seen comfort in before that time; my tongue I occupied with speech about Christ's Passion and rehearsing of the faith of Holy Church; and my heart I fastened on God, with all the trust and all the might that was in me. And I thought to myself, meaning: 'Thou hast now great busy-ness. If thou wouldst now from this time evermore be so busy to keep thee from sin, this were a sovereign and a good occupation.' For I believe truly, were I safe from sin I were full safe from all the fiends of hell and enemies of my soul.

Thus they kept me occupied all the night, and on the morrow till it was about the hour of prime. Then anon they were all gone and past, and there remained nothing but the stench and that lasted still a while. And I scorned them. In this way was I delivered of them by the virtue of Christ's Passion, 'for therewith is the fiend overcome', as Christ said before to me.

'Ah, wretched sin! What art thou? Thou art naught. For I saw that God is all thing—I saw not thee. And when I saw that God has made all thing I saw thee not, and when I saw that God is in all thing I saw thee not, and when I saw that God does all thing that is done, small and great, I saw thee not. And when I saw our Lord sit in our soul so worshipfully and love and like, rule and care for all that He has made, I saw not thee. Thus I am sure that thou art naught, and all those who love thee and like thee and follow thee and wilfully end in thee—I am sure they shall be brought to naught with thee and endlessly confounded. God shield us all from thee! So be it, for God's love.'

What wretchedness is I will say as I am taught by the shewing of God. Wretchedness is all thing that is not good: the ghostly blindness that we fall into in our first sin, and all that follows from that wretchedness, passions and pains, ghostly or bodily, and all that is on earth or in any other place which is not good.

And from this it may be asked, 'What are we?' And I answer to this: 'If all were departed from us that is not good; we should be good. When wretchedness is departed from us God and the soul is all one, and God and man all one.'

Does everything on earth thus divide us? I answer and say: 'In that it serves us, it is good, and in that it shall perish it is wretchedness; and in that man sets his heart upon it otherwise than in this way, it is sin.' And for the time that a man or woman loves sin (if there be any such), he is in pain that surpasses all pains. When he loves not sin but hates it and loves God, all is well; and he that truly does this though he sin sometimes through frailty or ignorance, yet in his will he falls not because he wills mightily to rise again and behold God whom he loves in all his will. God has made them (i.e. such men and women) to be loved by him or her that has been a sinner, but ever He loves and ever He longs to have our love. And when we mightily and wisely love Jesus, we are in peace.

All the blessed teaching of our Lord God was shewed to me in three parts, as I have said before. That is to say: by the bodily sight, and by words formed in my understanding, and by ghostly sight. For the bodily sight, I have said what I saw, as truly as I can. And for the words formed, I have said them right as our Lord shewed me them. And for the ghostly sight I have said somewhat, but I may never fully tell it. And therefore of this ghostly sight I am stirred to say more, as God will give me grace.

XXIV

LOVE MAKES MIGHT AND WISDOM FULL MEEK TO US

God shewed me two manner of sickness that we have, of which He wills that we be cured. The one is impatience, for we bear our travail and our pain heavily; the other is despair or doubtful dread, as I shall say afterwards. These two sicknesses are what most travail and tempest us (according to what our Lord shewed me), and what He most desires should be healed. I speak of such men and women as hate sin for God's love, and dispose themselves to do God's will. When this is so these two secret sins are the ones that most beset us. Therefore it is God's will that they be known, for then we shall refuse them as we do other sins.

Thus full meekly our Lord shewed me the patience that He had in His hard Passion, and also the joy and the liking that He takes in that Passion, out of love. This He did to shew us that we should gladly and easily bear our pains—for that is great pleasing to Him, and endless profit to us.

The reason why we are travailed by our pains is because of our unknowing of Love. Though the Persons of the Blessed Trinity are all equal in property, Love was most shewed to me in that it is most near to us all. And to the knowledge of this Love we are most blind. For many men and women believe that God is All-Mighty and *may* do all; and that He is All-Wisdom and *can* do all. But that He is All-Love and *will* do all—there they stop short. And this unknowing it is that most hinders God's lovers. For when they begin to hate sin and to amend their lives according to the ordinances of Holy Church, yet there remains a dread that stirs them to the beholding of self and of past sins. And this they take for humility, but it is a foul blindness and weakness which we are unable to despise. Yet if we really knew it we would immediately reject it as we do any other sin which we know: for it comes from the enemy and is against the truth.

For of all the properties of the Blessed Trinity it is God's will that we have most trust in liking and love; for Love makes Might and Wisdom full meek to us. And just as by the courtesy of God He forgets our sins from the time that we repent of them, right so He wills that we too forget our sins and all our doubtful dreads.

XV

GOD EVER WILLS THAT WE BE SECURE IN LOVE

FOR I saw four manner of dreads. One is the dread of fright that comes on a man suddenly, through frailty. This dread is good, for it helps to purge a man as does bodily sickness or other such pain that is not sinful; all such pains help man if they be patiently borne.

The second is dread of pain, whereby a man is roused and wakened from the sleep of sin. For a man who is sound asleep in sin is not able for the time to receive the soft comfort of the Holy Ghost until he has conceived this dread of the pain of bodily death and of the fire of purgatory. This dread rouses him to seek comfort and mercy from God, and thus this dread helps him as a means of approach to God, and enables him to have contrition through the blissful teaching of the Holy Ghost.

The third is a doubtful dread. Though it be little in itself, it is a species of despair, if the truth were known. For I am sure that God hates all doubtful dreads, and wills that we drive them from us by knowing of true Life.

The fourth is reverent dread. There is no dread that pleases Him in us but reverent dread, and that is full sweet and soft through the greatness of our love. Yet this reverent dread and love are not one and the same thing: they are two in property and in working but neither may be had without the other. Therefore I am sure that he who loves, dreads, though he may feel it but little.

All dreads other than reverent dread that are proffered to us, though they come under the colour of holiness are not so in truth, and hereby may they be known, which is which: this reverent dread, the more it is had the more it softens and comforts and pleases and rests the soul; and the false dread travails and distresses and troubles it. Then is this the remedy: to know them both and reject the false dread, just as we would do with a wicked spirit that shewed himself in the likeness of a good angel. For right as an evil spirit, though he come under the colour and the likeness of a good angel—though he shew himself in his pleasing talk and working ever so fair at first—yet he travails and distresses and troubles the person that he speaks with, hinders him and leaves him altogether in unrest. And the more such an evil spirit communes with the soul the more he travails him and the farther that soul is from peace. Therefore it is God's will, and to our own benefit, that we know them thus apart.

For God ever wills that we be secure in love and peaceful and restful, as He is to us. Just as He is to us, so wills He that we be to ourselves, and to our fellow-Christians. Amen.

Explicit Juliane de Norwych

POSTSCRIPT

AN EXCERPT FROM THE LONGER VERSION OF THE *REVELATIONS*

The following pages, some of the most beautiful and consoling in the whole of Julian's book, contain her development of the theme 'God is our Mother'. The theme, less well-known today than in the Middle Ages, is said to owe its diffusion, perhaps even its initiation, to Saint Anselm (1033–1109).[38] Julian's exquisite elaboration is an attempt on her part to bring home to her fellow-Christians the reality, intimacy and tenderness of God's 'homely loving'.

The excerpt consists of Chapters 59, 60 and 61 of the *Revelations*, newly transcribed and partially modernized from the sixteenth-century Paris manuscript.

All this bliss we have by Mercy and Grace, and such manner of bliss we might never have had nor known, had not that property of Goodness which is in God been opposed; it is because it was opposed that we have this bliss. For wickedness hath been suffered to rise up against the Goodness, and the Goodness of Mercy and Grace overcame that wickedness and turned all to goodness and worship for all that shall be saved (for Goodness is that property in God which doth good against evil).

Thus Jesus Christ, that doth good against evil, is our Very Mother. We have our being of Him, for there the Ground of Motherhood beginneth, with all the sweet keeping of Love that endlessly followeth. As truly as God is our Father, so truly is God our Mother; that showed He in all, and especially in these sweet words where He saith: 'I it am.' That is to say, 'I it am—the Might and the Goodness of Fatherhood. I it am—the Wisdom and the Kindliness of Motherhood. I it am—the Light and the Grace that is all blessed Love. I it am—the Trinity. I it am—the Unity. I it am—the high, sovereign Goodness of all manner of things. I it am that maketh thee to long. I it am—the endless fulfilling of all true desires.'

For there the soul is highest, noblest and most worshipful, and yet lowest, meekest and most mild. Of this Substantial Ground we have all our virtues; in our sensuality,[39] by the gift of Kind, and supernatural virtue by the helping and speeding of Mercy and Grace, without which we may profit nothing.

Our high Father, Almighty God, who is Being, He knoweth us and loveth us from before the beginning of time. Of this knowing, in His full, marvellous, deep charity, by the foreseeing endless counsel of all the blessed Trinity, He willed that the Second Person should become our Mother, our Brother and our Saviour. Wherefore it followeth that as truly as God is our Father so truly is God our Mother. Our Father willeth; our Mother worketh; our good Lord the Holy Ghost confirmeth. Therefore it belongeth to us to love our God, in whom we have our being, Him reverently thanking and praising for creating us, mightily praying to our Mother for mercy and pity, and to our Lord the Holy Ghost for help and grace.

For in these three is all our life: Kind, Mercy and Grace. Because of these we have mildness, patience and pity; and hatred of sin and wickedness (for it belongeth properly to virtue to hate sin and wickedness).

Thus is Jesus our true Mother according to Nature, because He, being God, created us; and He is our true Mother according to Grace, by His taking of our created nature. All the fair working and all the sweet, kindly offices of dearworthy Motherhood are appropriated to the Second Person, for in Him we have this goodly will whole and safe without end both by Nature and Grace, through His own proper goodness.

I understood three ways of beholding Motherhood in God. The first is grounded on His creation of our nature. The second is the taking of our nature—and there the Motherhood of Grace begins. The third is Motherhood of Working—in this is a forthspreading without end by the same Grace, in length and breadth, height and deepness. And all is one Love.

But now it behoves me to say a little more about this forthspreading as I understood it in the meaning of our Lord: how that we are brought again by the Motherhood of Mercy and Grace unto the perfection in which we were created by the Motherhood of kind love, which kind love never leaveth us.

Our kind Mother, our gracious Mother, because He willed wholly to become our Mother in all things, He laid the foundation of His work low and full mildly in the Virgin's womb. (And that shewed He in the First Revelation, where He brought that meek Maid before the eye of my understanding, in her simple stature, as she was when she conceived.) That is to say, our high God, the sovereign Wisdom of all, in this humble place He arrayed and robed Himself in our poor flesh all ready to do Himself the services and the office of Motherhood in all things.

The Mother's service is nearest, readiest and surest: nearest, for it is closest to nature; readiest, for it is most full of love; and surest, for it is most true. This office none might, nor could ever anyone do to the full, but only He.

We know that all our mothers bear us unto pain and dying. What is that? But our Very Mother, Jesus, He alone beareth us unto joy and to endless living, blessed may He be! Thus He carries us within Him in love and travail until the full time; when He willed to suffer the sharpest thorns and most grievous pains that ever were or shall be, and died at last. And when He had done thus and so borne us to bliss, yet might not all this fully satisfy His marvellous love—that shewed He in these high, overpassing words of love: 'If I might suffer more, I would suffer more.'

He might no more die, but He would not leave off working. It behoved Him, therefore, to fend for us, for the dearworthy love of Motherhood hath made Him debtor to us. The mother may give her child suck of her milk, but our precious Mother, Jesus, He may feed us with Himself, and doth—full courteously and full tenderly—with the Blessed Sacrament, that is the precious food of true life; and with all the sweet Sacraments He sustaineth us full mercifully and graciously. Thus meant He in these blessed words where He said: 'I it am that Holy Church preacheth thee and teacheth thee.' That is to say: 'All the virtue and the grace of my word, all the goodness that is ordained in Holy Church for thee, I it am.' The Mother may fold her child tenderly to her breast, but our tender Mother, Jesus, He may homely lead us into His blessed Breast by His sweet open side, and give us therein a glimpse of the Godhead and the joys of heaven, with ghostly sureness of endless bliss. And that shewed He in the Ninth Revelation, giving the same understanding in this sweet word where He saith: 'Lo! how I love thee', while He looked down at His blessed side, rejoicing.

This fair, lovely word, *Mother*, it is so sweet and so kindly in itself, that it cannot full truly be said of anyone or to anyone but of Him and to Him who is Very Mother of life and of all. To the property of Motherhoood belongeth kind love, wisdom and knowing, and it is good. For though it be so that our bodily forth-bringing be but little, low and simple in the light of our ghostly bringing forth, yet it is He that doth it in the creatures by whom it is done. A kind, loving mother knoweth and understandeth the needs of her child. She keeps it very tenderly, as the nature and condition of motherhood will; and ever as it groweth in age and stature, she changeth her working but not her love. And when it has grown still more she permits that it be chastised (unto the breaking down of vices) to make the child receive virtues and graces. This working, with all that be fair and good, our Lord doth in those by whom it is done. Thus He is our Mother according to Nature, by the working of Grace in the lower part for the sake of the higher; and He wills that we know this, for He will have all our love fastened to Him.

In this I saw that all the debt we owe by God's bidding, to Fatherhood and Motherhood, is fulfilled in true loving of God; which blessed love Christ worketh in us. And this was shewed in all and especially in the high plenteous words where He saith: 'I it am that thou lovest.'

By as much as our soul is of more price in His sight so in our ghostly bringing forth He useth more tenderness in keeping us, without any comparison. He kindleth our understanding. He prepareth our ways. He easeth our conscience. He comforteth our soul. He lighteneth our heart and giveth us, in part, knowing and loving of His blessed Godhead, with gracious mind in His sweet Manhood and His blessed Passion, with courteous marvelling in His high, overpassing Goodness. He maketh us to love all that He loveth, for His love, and to be well pleased with Him and with all His works. And when we fall, swiftly He raiseth us by His loving clasp and His gracious touching. When we are strengthened by His sweet working then we wilfully choose Him, by His grace, to be His servants and His lovers lastingly, without end.

Yet, after this, He suffereth some of us to fall more deeply and more grievously than ever we did before, as it seemeth to us. Then think we (who be not all wise!) that all has come to naught that we had begun. But it is not so. For it is needful for us to fall, and it is needful for us to see it. For if we fell not, we should not know how feeble and how wretched we are of ourselves; nor would we know so fully the marvellous love of our Maker.

For we shall see truly in heaven, without end, that we have sinned grievously in this life, and notwithstanding this, we shall see truly that we were never hurt in His love, nor ever the less precious in His sight. And by the experience of this falling we shall have a high, marvellous knowing of love in God, without end. For staunch and marvellous is that love which cannot and will not be broken by trespass. This was one understanding of profit. Another is the lowness and meekness that we shall get by the sight of our falling; for by this we shall be raised high in heaven, and we might never have come to be raised thus high without that meekness. Therefore it is needful for us to see it: for if we see it not, though we fell it would not profit us. And commonly first we fall and afterwards we see it, and both through the Mercy of God.

A mother may allow her child to fall sometimes and to be distressed in various ways for its own profit. But she may never permit any manner of peril to befall her child, out of love. And even though our earthly mother may permit her child to perish, our heavenly Mother, Jesus, can never suffer us who are His children to perish. For He is All-Mighty, All-Wisdom and All-Love, and so is none but He, blessed may He be!

But often-times when our falling and our wretchedness are shewed to us, we are so sore adread and so greatly ashamed of ourselves that we scarcely know where to put ourselves. Then our courteous Mother wills not that we flee away—nothing could be more displeasing to Him. No, He willeth that we use then the ways of a child, for when it is distressed and afeard it runneth with haste to its mother and, if it can do nothing else, it crieth out with all its might to the mother, for help. So will He that we act like a meek child, saying thus: 'My kind

Mother, my gracious Mother, my dearworthy Mother, have mercy on me. I have made myself foul and unlike to Thee, and I neither may nor can amend except with Thy help and grace.' And if we be not eased at once, let us be sure that He is using the behaviour of a wise mother. For if He seeth that it be profitable for us to mourn and to weep, He permitteth it, with ruth and pity, for love, unto the best time. And He willeth then that we use the property of a child that evermore trusteth naturally to the love of its mother in weal and in woe.

He willeth too, that we betake us mightily to the Faith of Holy Church, and find there our dearworthy Mother in solace and true understanding with all the communion of the blessed. For one single person may often-times be broken, as it seemeth to itself, but the whole Body of Holy Church was never broken, nor ever shall be without end. It is therefore a sure thing, a good and gracious thing, to will meekly and mightily to be fastened and oned to our Mother, Holy Church, that is, Christ Jesus. For the flood of mercy that is His dearworthy blood and precious water is plenteous enough to make us fair and clean; the blessed wounds of our Saviour are open and rejoice to heal us; the sweet gracious hands of our Mother are ready and diligent about us. For He, in all this working, useth the very office of a kindly nurse that hath nothing else to do but attend to the salvation of her child. It is His office to save us. It is His glory to do it. And it is His will that we know this. For He willeth that we love Him sweetly and trust in Him meekly and mightily. And this shewed He in these gracious words: 'I keep thee full surely.'

NOTES

1. Five manuscripts of *Sixteen Revelations of Divine Love* are known to us, of which four are in London and one in Paris.

   In order of age they rank as follows:—

   (*i*) British Museum Additional MS. 37790, mid-fifteenth century.

   (*ii*) Westminster Cathedral Manuscript, late fifteenth or early sixteenth century.

   (*iii*) Bibliothèque Nationale, Paris, Fonds Anglais, 40, sixteenth century.

   (*iv*) British Museum Sloane MS. 2499, mid-seventeenth century.

   (*v*) British Museum Sloane MS. 3705, late seventeenth or early eighteenth century.

   The Paris and both Sloane manuscripts contain substantially the same subject-matter and are almost equal in length, while the Westminster manuscript contains extracts only from the *Revelations* and appears to derive ultimately from the same source as the Paris manuscript.
2. Sister Anna Maria Reynolds, C.P., 'Some Literary Influences in the *Revelations* of Julian of Norwich', *Leeds Studies in English and Kindred Languages*, Nos. 7 and 8, 1952, p. 18.
3. See Eileen Power, *Medieval English Nunneries* (Cambridge 1922), p. 260.
4. So Father James Walsh, S.J., in a paper on 'The Johannine Doctrine of Indwelling in the *Revelations* of Julian of Norwich' (Rome 1956).

5. *Cambridge Medieval History*, VII, 807.
6. R. W. Chambers, *On the Continuity of English Prose* (London 1932), p. cxvii.
7. Dom D. Knowles, *The English Mystics* (London 1927), p. 148.
8. Chambers, op. cit., p. cvii.
9. H. Read, *English Prose Style* (London 1928), p. 99.
10. H. E. Allen, *The English Writings of Richard Rolle* (Oxford 1931), pp. lviii–lix.
11. Knowles, op. cit., p. 62.
12. Cf. F. D. S. Darwin, *The English Medieval Recluse* (London, no date), pp. 5–6.
13. See *The Ancrene Riwle*, Rendered into Modern English and edited by M. B. Salu (London 1955), pp. xxiii–xxiv. Quotations from the *Riwle* are taken from this edition.
14. Cf. Darwin, op. cit., pp. 42–52, 71–78.
15. R. M. Clay, 'Further Studies on Medieval Recluses', *Journal of the British Archæological Association*, Third Series, XVI, p. 74.
16. Ibid. pp. 75ff. See also W. A. Pantin, *The English Church in the Fourteenth Century* (Cambridge 1955), pp. 245–247.
17. H. E. Allen, *Writings Ascribed to Richard Rolle, Hermit of Hampole, and Materials for His Biography* (New York 1927), p. 266.
18. Cf. Darwin, op. cit., p. 65.
19. Knowles, op. cit., p. 62.
20. For a detailed and scholarly answer to this question the reader is referred to a study by Father Paul Molinari, S.J., in which Julian's spiritual teaching is beautifully expounded and thoroughly vindicated:

Julian of Norwich: The Teaching of a Fourteenth Century English Mystic (London 1958).

21. Knowles, op. cit., pp. 16, 6.
22. Cf. 1. Cor. 12: 3.
23. Quotations from the Works of St John of the Cross and St Teresa are taken from *The Complete Works of St John of the Cross* translated and edited by E. Allison Peers from the critical edition of P. Silverio de Santa Teresa, C.D. (London 1953, 3 vols.) and *The Complete Works of St Teresa of Jesus*, translated and edited by E. Allison Peers from the critical edition of P. Silverio de Santa Teresa, C.D. (London 1946, 3 vols.).
24. Very Rev. A. Tanquerey, *A Treatise on Ascetical and Mystical Theology*, translated by the Rev. H. Branderis S.S.A.M. (Tournai 1948), section 1480.
25. Tanquerey, op. cit., section 1419.
26. Cf. St Augustine, 'De Genesi ad Litteram', XII, vii (*Patrologia Latina* 34. col. 459).
27. Tanquerey, op. cit., section 1473.
28. See note 23 above.
29. *What . . . Love.* These words, omitted in the Paris MS., are taken from MS. Sloane 2499.
30. Two attractive editions of the Longer Version of the *Revelations* are available: that prepared by Dom R. Hudleston in the Orchard Series (London, second edition 1952) and that of Grace Warrack (London, fourteenth edition 1952).
31. Cf. Luke 1: 38.
32. St Gregory; cf. *Patrologia Latina* LXVI, col. 200.
33. Cf. Rom. 8: 35: Matthew 8: 25; 14: 30.
34. John 19; 28.
35. Cf. Phil., 2: 5.

36. The manuscript reads *whate* es any . . . but the *whate* is probably a scribal misreading of *whare* (where), which is the reading of the Longer Version.

37. Between Chapters XIX and XX of the Shorter Version is given the extra material contained in the Longer Text, Chapters 44–63. See Introduction, p. xii.

38. See André Cabassut, O.S.B., 'Une Dévotion Médiévale Peu Connue: La Dévotion à "Jésus notre Mère"', *Revue d'Ascétique et de Mystique*, 99–100, Avril-Décembre 1949. Cf. also Sister Anna Maria Reynolds, op. cit., p. 21, note 15.

39. The author of *The Cloud of Unknowing* defines 'sensuality' as 'a power of our soul, recking and reigning in the bodily wits, through the which we have bodily knowing and feeling of all bodily creatures, whether they be pleasing or unpleasing'. *The Cloud of Unknowing*, edited E. Underhill (London 1922), Ch. 66, p. 282.

GLOSSARY

Bodily	outward, visible, audible.
Dearworthy	dear, precious.
Doubtful	full of fears; doubtful dreads, fears due to excessive timidity.
Generally	universally, in general, to all alike.
Instrument	agent, intermediary.
Kind	(*noun*) nature; (*adj.*) natural, filial, dutiful.
Likes	(*impersonal verb*) is pleasing to; gives joy to.
Liking	joy, pleasure, satisfaction.
Mean	intend, have in mind.
Meed	reward.
Mind	memory, mindfulness, understanding of.
Property	characteristic quality of a person or thing; attribute.
Ruth	compassion, pity, sorrow.
Singularly	particularly, individually, in special.
Speed	(*verb*) help, further, benefit; (*noun*) a help, means of success.
Stir	move, incline, prompt, encourage, tempt.
Tempest	tempt, try sorely, upset.
Travail	(*verb*) cause anguish to, afflict grievously; (*noun*) acute suffering, anguish, distress, pain.
Wilful	willing, purposeful, earnest.
Worship	glory, honour.

APPENDIX

The following table indicates the chapters which correspond to each other in the longer and shorter versions of the *Revelations*.

	Longer Version	*Shorter Version*
Introductory; mainly biographical	1–3	I–III
The First Revelation	4–9	III–VII
The Second Revelation	10	VIII
The Third Revelation	11	VIII
The Fourth Revelation	12	VIII
The Fifth Revelation	13	VIII
The Sixth Revelation	14	IX
The Seventh Revelation	15	IX
The Eighth Revelation	16–21	X–XI
The Ninth Revelation	22–23	XII
The Tenth Revelation	24	XIII
The Eleventh Revelation	25	XIII
The Twelfth Revelation	26	XIII–XIV
The Thirteenth Revelation	27–40	XV–XVIII
The Fourteenth Revelation	41	XIX
The Fifteenth Revelation	64–65	XX
Tempested by the Fiend	66	XXI
The Sixteenth Revelation	67–68	XXII
The Fiend again	69	XXIII
Sundry Teachings	70–86	XXIII–XXV

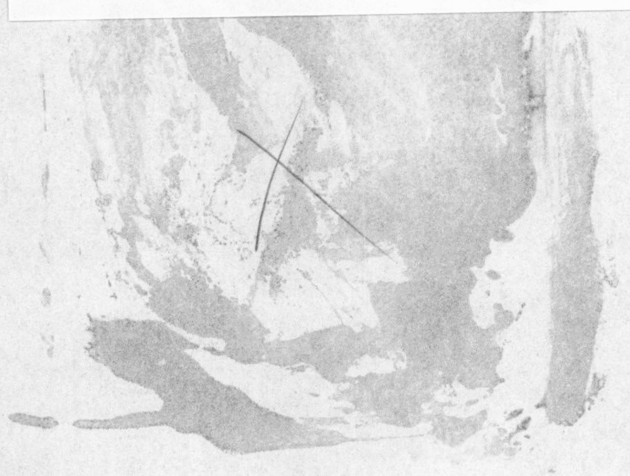